Clarel by Herman Melville

Part I – (of IV) Jerusalem

BY A SPONTANEOUS ACT, NOT VERY LONG AGO, MY KINSMAN, THE LATE PETER GANESEVOORT, OF ALBANY. N. Y., IN A PERSONAL INTERVIEW PROVIDED FOR THE PUBLICATION OF THIS POEM, KNOWN TO HIM BY REPORT, AS EXISTING IN MANUSCRIPT.

JUSTLY AND AFFECTIONATELY THE PRINTED BOOK IS INSCRIBED IN HIS NAME

Herman Melville was born in New York City on August 1st, 1819, the third of eight children.

At the age of 7 Melville contracted scarlet fever which was to permanently diminish his eyesight. At this time Melville was described as being "very backwards in speech and somewhat slow in comprehension."

His father died when he was 12 leaving the family in very straitened times. Just 14 Melville took a job in a bank paying $150 a year that he obtained via his uncle, Peter Gansevoort, who was one of the directors of the New York State Bank.

After a failed stint as a surveyor he signed on to go to sea and travelled across the Atlantic to Liverpool and then on further voyages to the Pacific on adventures which would soon become the architecture of his novels. Whilst travelling he joined a mutiny, was jailed, fell in love with a South Pacific beauty and became known as a figure of opposition to the coercion of native Hawaiians to the Christian religion.

He drew from these experiences in his books Typee, Omoo, and White-Jacket. These were published as novels, the first initially in London in 1846.

By 1851 his masterpiece, Moby Dick, was ready to be published. It is perhaps, and certainly at the time, one of the most ambitious novels ever written. However, it never sold out its initial print run of 3,000 and Melville's earnings on this masterpiece were a mere $556.37.

In succeeding years his reputation waned and he found life increasingly difficult. His family was growing, now four children, and a stable income was essential.

With his finances in a disappointing state Melville took the advice of friends that a change in career was called for. For many others public lecturing had proved very rewarding. From late 1857 to 1860, Melville embarked upon three lecture tours, where he spoke mainly on Roman statuary and sightseeing in Rome.

In 1876 he was at last able to publish privately his 16,000 line epic poem Clarel. It was to no avail. The book had an initial printing of 350 copies, but sales failed miserably.

On December 31st, 1885 Melville was at last able to retire. His wife had inherited several small legacies and provide them with a reasonable income.

Herman Melville, novelist, poet, short story writer and essayist, died at his home on September 28rh 1891 from cardiovascular disease.

Index of Contents

Canto I - The Hostel

In chamber low and scored by time,
Masonry old, late washed with lime—
Much like a tomb new-cut in stone;
Elbow on knee, and brow sustained
All motionless on sidelong hand,
A student sits, and broods alone.
The small deep casement sheds a ray
Which tells that in the Holy Town
It is the passing of the day—
The Vigil of Epiphany.
Beside him in the narrow cell
His luggage lies unpacked; thereon
The dust lies, and on him as well—
The dust of travel. But anon
His face he lifts—in feature fine,
Yet pale, and all but feminine
But for the eye and serious brow—
Then rises, paces to and fro,
And pauses, saying, "Other cheer
Than that anticipated here,

By me the learner, now I find.
Theology, art thou so blind?
What means this naturalistic knell
In lieu of Siloh's oracle
Which here should murmur?
Snatched from grace,
And waylaid in the holy place!
Not thus it was but yesterday
Off Jaffa on the clear blue sea;
Nor thus, my heart, it was with thee
Landing amid the shouts and spray;
Nor thus when mounted, full equipped,
Out through the vaulted gate we slipped
Beyond the walls where gardens bright
With bloom and blossom cheered the sight.
"The plain we crossed. In afternoon,
How like our early autumn bland—

So softly tempered for a boon—
The breath of Sharon's prairie land!
And was it, yes, her titled Rose,
That scarlet poppy oft at hand?
Then Ramleh gleamed, the sail white town
At even. There I watched day close
From the fair tower, the suburb one:
Seaward and dazing set the sun:
Inland I turned me toward the wall
Of Ephraim, stretched in purple pall.
Romance of mountains! But in end
What change the near approach could lend.
"The start this morning—gun and lance
Against the quarter moon's low tide;
The thieves' huts where we hushed the ride;
Chill daybreak in the lorn advance;
In stony strait the scorch of noon,
Thrown off-by crags, reminding one
Of those hot paynims whose fierce hands
Flung showers of Afric's fiery sands
In face of that crusader king,
Louis, to wither so his wing;
And, at the last, aloft for goal,
Like the ice bastions round the Pole,
Thy blank, blank towers, Jerusalem!"
Again he droops, with brow on hand.
But, starting up, "Why, well I knew
Salem to be no Samarcand;
'Twas scarce surprise; and yet first view
Brings this eclipse. Needs be my soul,
Purged by the desert's subtle air
From bookish vapors, now is heir
To nature's influx of control;
Comes likewise now to consciousness
Of the true import of that press
Of inklings which in travel late
Through Latin lands, did vex my state,
And somehow seemed clandestine. Ah!
These under formings in the mind,
Banked corals which ascend from far,
But little heed men that they wind
Unseen, unheard—till lo, the reef—
The reef and breaker, wreck and grief.
But here unlearning, how to me
Opes the expanse of time's vast sea!
Yes, I am young, but Asia old.
The books, the books not all have told.
"And, for the rest, the facile chat

Of overweenings—what was that
The grave one said in Jaffa lane
Whom there I met, my countryman,
But new returned from travel here;
Some word of mine provoked the strain;
His meaning now begins to clear:
Let me go over it again:—
"Our New World's worldly wit so shrewd
Lacks the Semitic reverent mood,
Unworldly—hardly may confer
Fitness for just interpreter
Of Palestine. Forego the state
Of local minds inveterate,
Tied to one poor and casual form.
To avoid the deep saves not from storm.
"Those things he said, and added more;
No clear authenticated lore
I deemed. But now, need now confess
My cultivated narrowness,
Though scarce indeed of sort he meant?
'Tis the uprooting of content!"
So he, the student. 'Twas a mind,
Earnest by nature, long confined
Apart like Vesta in a grove
Collegiate, but let to rove
At last abroad among mankind,
And here in end confronted so
By the true genius, friend or foe,
And actual visage of a place
Before but dreamed of in the glow
Of fancy's spiritual grace.
Further his meditations aim,
Reverting to his different frame
Bygone. And then: "Can faith remove
Her light, because of late no plea
I've lifted to her source above?"
Dropping thereat upon the knee,
His lips he parted; but the word
Against the utterance demurred
And failed him. With infirm intent
He sought the housetop. Set of sun:
His feet upon the yet warm stone,
He, Clarel, by the coping leant,
In silent gaze. The mountain town,
A walled and battlemented one,
With houseless suburbs front and rear,
And flanks built up from steeps severe,
Saddles and turrets the ascent—

Tower which rides the elephant.
Hence large the view. There where he stood,
Was Acra's upper neighborhood.
The circling hills he saw, with one
Excelling, ample in its crown,
Making the uplifted city low
By contrast—Olivet. The flow
Of eventide was at full brim;
Overlooked, the houses sloped from him—
Terraced or domed, unchimnied, gray,
All stone—a moor of roofs. No play
Of life; no smoke went up, no sound
Except low hum, and that half drowned.
The inn abutted on the pool
Named Hezekiah's, a sunken court
Where silence and seclusion rule,
Hemmed round by walls of nature's sort,
Base to stone structures seeming one
E'en with the steeps they stand upon.
As a threedecker's sternlights peer
Down on the oily wake below,
Upon the sleek dark waters here
The inn's small lattices bestow
A rearward glance. And here and there
In flaws the languid evening air
Stirs the dull weeds adust, which trail
In festoons from the crag, and veil
The ancient fissures, overtopped
By the tall convent of the Copt,
Built like a lighthouse o'er the main.
Blind arches showed in walls of wane,
Sealed windows, portals masoned fast,
And terraces where nothing passed
By parapets all dumb. No tarn
Among the Kaatskills, high above
Farmhouse and stack, last lichened barn
And logbridge rotting in remove—
More lonesome looks than this dead pool
In town where living creatures rule.
Not here the spell might he undo;
The strangeness haunted him and grew.
But twilight closes. He descends
And toward the inner court he wends.

Canto II - Abdon

A lamp in archway hangs from key—
A lamp whose sidelong rays are shed
On a slim vial set in bed
Of doorpost all of masonry.
That vial hath the Gentile vexed;
Within it holds Talmudic text,
Or charm. And there the Black Jew sits,
Abdon the host. The lamplight flits
O'er reverend beard of saffron hue
Sweeping his robe of Indian blue.
Disturbed and troubled in estate,
Longing for solacement of mate,
Clarel in court there nearer drew,
As yet unnoted, for the host
In meditation seemed engrossed,
Perchance upon some line late scanned
In leathern scroll that drooped from hand.
Ere long, without surprise expressed,
The lone man marked his lonelier guest,
And welcomed him. Discourse was bred;
In end a turn it took, and led
To grave recital. Here was one
(If question of his word be none)
Descended from those dubious men,
The unreturning tribes, the Ten
Whom shout and halloo wide have sought,
Lost children in the wood of time.
Yes, he, the Black Jew, stinting naught,
Averred that ancient India's clime
Harbored the remnant of the Tribes,
A people settled with their scribes
In far Cochin. There was he born
And nurtured, and there yet his kin,
Never from true allegiance torn,
Kept Moses' law.
            Cochin, Cochin
(Mused Clarel). I have heard indeed
Of those Black Jews, their ancient creed
And hoar tradition. Esdras saith
The Ten Tribes built in Arsareth—
Eastward, still eastward. That may be.
But look, the scroll of goatskin, see
Wherein he reads, a wizard book;
It is the Indian Pentateuch
Whereof they tell. Whate'er the plea
(And scholars various notions hold
Touching these missing clans of old),
This seems a deeper mystery;

How Judah, Benjamin, live on—
Unmixed into time's swamping sea
So far can urge their Amazon.
He pondered. But again the host,
Narrating part his lifetime tossed,
Told how, long since, with trade in view,
He sailed from India with a Jew
And merchant of the Portuguese
For Lisbon. More he roved the seas
And marts, till in the last event
He pitched in Amsterdam his tent.
"There had I lived my life," he said,
"Among my kind, for good they were;
But loss came loss, and I was led
To long for Judah—only her.
But see." He rose, and took the light
And led within: "There ye espy
What prospect's left to such as I—
Yonder!"—a dark slab stood upright
Against the wall; a rude gravestone
Sculptured, with Hebrew ciphers strown.
"Under Moriah it shall lie
No distant date, for very soon,
Ere yet a little, and I die.
From Ind to Zion have I come,
But less to live, than end at home.
One other last remove!" he sighed,
And meditated on the stone,
Lamp held aloft. That magnified
The hush throughout the dim unknown
Of night—night in a land how dead!
Thro' Clarel's heart the old man's strain
Dusky meandered in a vein
One with the revery it bred;
His eyes still dwelling on the Jew
In added dream—so strange his shade
Of swartness like a born Hindoo,
And wizened visage which betrayed
The Hebrew cast. And subtile yet
In ebon frame an amulet
Which on his robe the patriarch wore—
And scroll, and vial in the door,
These too contributed in kind.
They parted. Clarel sought his cell
Or tomblike chamber, and—with mind
To break or intermit the spell,
At least perplex it and impede—
Lighted the lamp of olive oil,

And, brushing from a trunk the soil—
'Twas one late purchased at his need—
Opened, and strove to busy him
With small adjustments. Bootless cheer!
While wavering now, in chanceful skim
His eyes fell on the word JUDEA
In paper lining of the tray,
For all was trimmed, in cheaper way,
With printed matter. Curious then
To know this faded denizen,
He read, and found a piece complete,
Briefly comprised in one poor sheet:

"The World accosts—

"Last one out of Holy Land,
What gift bring'st thou? Sychem grapes?
Tabor, which the Eden drapes,
Yieldeth garlands. I demand
Something cheery at thy hand.
Come, if Solomon's Song thou singest,
Haply Sharon's rose thou bringest."

"The Palmer replies:

"Nay, naught thou nam'st thy servant brings,
Only Judea my feet did roam;
And mainly there the pilgrim clings
About the precincts of Christ's tomb.
These palms I bring—from dust not free,
Since dust and ashes both were trod by me.
O'er true thy gift (thought Clarel).
Well, Scarce might the world accept, 'twould seem.
But I, shall I my feet impel
Through road like thine and naught redeem?
Rather thro' brakes, lone brakes,
I wind: As I advance they close behind.—
Thought's burden! on the couch he throws
Himself and it—rises, and goes
To peer from casement. 'Twas moonlight,
With stars, the Olive Hill in sight,
Distinct, yet dreamy in repose,
As of Katahdin in hot noon,
Lonely, with all his pines in swoon.
The nature and evangel clashed,
Rather, a double mystery flashed.
Olivet, Olivet do I see?
The ideal upland, trod by Thee?

Up or reclined, he felt the soul
Afflicted by that noiseless calm,
Till sleep, the good nurse, deftly stole
The bed beside, and for a charm
Took the pale hand within her own,
Nor left him till the night was gone.

Canto III - The Sepulchre

In Crete they claimed the tomb of Jove
In glen over which his eagles soar;
But thro' a peopled town ye rove
To Christ's low urn, where, nigh the door,
Settles the dove. So much the more
The contrast stamps the human God
Who dwelt among us, made abode
With us, and was of woman born;
Partook our bread, and thought no scorn
To share the humblest, homeliest hearth,
Shared all of man except the sin and mirth.
Such, among thronging thoughts, may stir
In pilgrim pressing thro' the lane
That dusty wins the reverend fane,
Seat of the Holy Sepulchre,
And naturally named therefrom.
What altars old in cluster rare
And grotto shrines engird the Tomb:
Caves and a crag; and more is there;
And halls monastic join their gloom.
To sum in comprehensive bounds
The Passion's drama with its grounds,
Immense the temple winds and strays
Finding each storied precinct out—
Absorbs the sites all roundabout—
Omnivorous, and a world of maze.
And yet time was when all here stood
Separate, and from rood to rood,
Chapel to shrine, or tent to tent,
Unsheltered still the pilgrim went
Where now enroofed the whole coheres—
Where now thro' influence of years
And spells by many a legend lent,
A sort of nature reappears—
Sombre or sad, and much in tone
Perhaps with that which here was known
Of yore, when from this Salem height,

Then sylvan in primeval plight,
Down came to Shaveh's Dale, with wine
And bread, after the four Kings' check,
The Druid priest Melchizedek,
Abram to bless with rites divine.
What rustlings here from shadowy spaces,
Deep vistas where the votary paces,
Will, strangely intermitting, creep
Like steps in Indian forest deep.
How birdlike steals the singer's note
Down from some rail or arch remote:
While, glimmering where kneelers be,
Small lamps, dispersed, with glowworm light
Mellow the vast nave's azure night,
And make a haze of mystery:
The blur is spread of thousand years,
And Calvary's seen as through one's tears.
In cloistral walks the dome detains
Hermits, which during public days
Seclude them where the shadow stays,
But issue when charmed midnight reigns,
Unshod, with tapers lit, and roam,
According as their hearts appoint,
The purlieus of the central Tomb
In round of altars; and anoint
With fragrant oils each marble shelf;
Or, all alone, strange solace find
And oratory to their mind
Lone locked within the Tomb itself.
Cells note ye as in bower a nest
Where some sedate rich devotee
Or grave guest monk from over sea
Takes up through Lent his votive rest,
Adoring from his saintly perch
Golgotha and the guarded Urn,
And mysteries everywhere expressed;
Until his soul, in rapt sojourn,
Add one more chapel to the Church.
The friars in turn which tend the Fane,
Dress it and keep, a home make there
Nor pass for weeks the gate. Again
Each morning they ascend the stair
Of Calvary, with cloth and broom,
For dust thereon will settle down,
And gather, too, upon the Tomb
And places of the Passion's moan.
Tradition, not device and fraud
Here rules—tradition old and broad.

Transfixed in sites the drama's shown—
Each given spot assigned; 'tis here
They scourged Him; soldiers yonder nailed
The Victim to the tree; in jeer
There stood the Jews; there Mary paled;
The vesture was divided here.
A miracle play of haunted stone—
A miracle play, a phantom one,
With power to give pause or subdue.
So that whatever comment be
Serious, if to faith unknown—
Not possible seems levity
Or aught that may approach thereto.
And, sooth, to think what numbers here,
Age after age, have worn the stones
In suppliance or judgment fear;
What mourners—men and women's moans,
Ancestors of ourselves indeed;
What souls whose penance of remorse
Made poignant by the elder creed,
Found honest language in the force
Of chains entwined that ate the bone;
How here a' Becket's slayers clung
Taking the contrite anguish on,
And, in release from fast and thong,
Buried upon Moriah sleep;
With more, much more; such ties, so deep,
Endear the spot, or false or true
As an historic site. The wrong
Of carpings never may undo
The nerves that clasp about the plea
Tingling with kinship through and through—
Faith childlike and the tried humanity.
But little here moves hearts of some;
Rather repugnance grave, or scorn
Or cynicism, to mark the dome
Beset in court or yard forlorn
By pedlars versed in wonted tricks,
Venders of charm or crucifix;
Or, on saint days, to hark the din
As during market day at inn,
And polyglot of Asian tongues
And island ones, in interchange
Buzzed out by crowds in costumes strange
Of nations divers. Are these throngs Merchants?
Is this Cairo's bazar And concourse?
Nay, thy strictures bar. It is but simple nature, see;
None mean irreverence, though free.

Unvexed by Europe's grieving doubt
Which asks And can the Father be?
Those children of the climes devout,
On festival in fane installed,
Happily ignorant, make glee
Like orphans in the playground walled.
Others the duskiness may find
Imbued with more than nature's gloom;
These, loitering hard by the Tomb,
Alone, and when the day's declined—
So that the shadow from the stone
Whereon the angel sat is thrown
To distance more, and sigh or sound
Echoes from place of Mary's moan,
Or cavern where the cross was found;
Or mouse stir steals upon the ear
From where the soldier reached the spear—
Shrink, much like Ludovico erst
Within the haunted chamber. Thou,
Less sensitive, yet haply versed
In everything above, below—
In all but thy deep human heart;
Thyself perchance mayst nervous start
At thine own fancy's final range
Who here wouldst mock: with mystic smart
The subtile Eld can slight avenge.
But gibe—gibe on, until there crawl
About thee in the scorners' seat,
Reactions; and pride's Smyrna shawl
Plague strike the wearer. Ah, retreat!
But how of some which still deplore
Yet share the doubt? Here evermore
'Tis good for such to turn afar
From the Skull's place, even Golgotha,
And view the cedarn dome in sun
Pierced like the marble Pantheon:
No blurring pane, but open sky:
In there day peeps, there stars go by,
And, in still hours which these illume,
Heaven's dews drop tears upon the Tomb.
Nor lack there dreams romance can thrill:
In hush when tides and towns are still,
Godfrey and Baldwin from their graves
(Made meetly near the rescued Stone)
Rise, and in arms. With beaming glaives
They watch and ward the urn they won.
So fancy deals, a light achiever:
Imagination, earnest ever,

Recalls the Friday far away,
Relives the crucifixion day—
The passion and its sequel proves,
Sharing the three pale Marys' frame;
Thro' the eclipse with these she moves
Back to the house from which they came
To Golgotha. O empty room, O leaden heaviness of doom—
O cowering hearts, which sore beset
Deem vain the promise now, and yet
Invoke him who returns no call;
And fears for more that may befall.
O terror linked with love which cried
"Art gone? is't o'er? and crucified?"
Who might foretell from such dismay
Of blank recoilings, all the blest
Lilies and anthems which attest
The floral Easter holiday?

Canto IV - Of the Crusaders

When sighting first the towers afar
Which girt the object of the war
And votive march—the Saviour's Tomb,
What made the redeross knights so shy?
And wherefore did they doff the plume
And baldrick, kneel in dust, and sigh?
Hardly it serves to quote Voltaire
And say they were freebooters—hence,
Incapable of awe or sense
Pathetic; no, for man is heir
To complex moods; and in that age
Belief devout and bandit rage
Frequent were joined; and e'en today
At shrines on the Calabrian steep—
Not insincere while feelings sway—
The brigand halts to adore, to weep.
Grant then the worst—is all romance
Which claims that the crusader's glance
Was blurred by tears?
But if that round
Of disillusions which accrue
In this our day, imply a ground
For more concern than Tancred knew,
Thinking, yet not as in despair,
Of Christ who suffered for him there
Upon the crag; then, own it true,

Cause graver much than his is ours
At least to check the hilarious heart
Before these memorable towers.
But wherefore this? such theme why start?
Because if here in many a place
The rhyme—much like the knight indeed—
Abjure brave ornament, 'twill plead
Just reason, and appeal for grace.

Canto V - Clarel

Upon the morrow's early morn
Clarel is up, and seeks the Urn.
Advancing towards the fane's old arch
Of entrance—curved in sculptured stone,
Dim and defaced, he saw thereon
From rural Bethany the march
Of Christ into another gate—
The golden and triumphal one,
Upon Palm Morn. For porch to shrine
On such a site, how fortunate
That adaptation of design.
Well might it please.
He entered then.
Strangers were there, of each degree,
From Asian shores, with island men,
Mild guests of the Epiphany.
As when to win the Paschal joy
And Nisan's festal month renew, The
Nazarenes to temple drew,
Even Joseph, Mary, and the BOY,
Whose hand the mother's held; so here
To later rites and altars dear,
Domestic in devotion's flame
Husbands with wives and children came.
But he, the student, under dome
Pauses; he stands before the Tomb.
Through open door he sees the wicks
Alight within, where six and six
For Christ's apostles, night and day,
Lamps, olden lamps do burn. In smoke
Befogged they shed no vivid ray,
But heat the cell and seem to choke.
He marked, and revery took flight:
"These burn not like those aspects bright
Of starry watchers when they kept

Vigil at napkined feet and head
Of Him their Lord.—Nay, is He fled?
Or tranced lies, tranced nor unbewept
With Dorian gods? or, fresh and clear,
A charm diffused throughout the sphere,
Streams in the ray through yonder dome?
Not hearsed He is. But hath ghost home
Dispersed in soil, in sea, in air?
False Pantheism, false though fair!"
So he; and slack and aimless went,
Nor might untwine the ravelment
Of doubts perplexed. For easement there
Halting awhile in pillared shade,
A friar he marked, in robe of blue
And round Greek cap of sable hue:
Poor men he led; much haste he made,
Nor sequence kept, but dragged them so
Hither and thither, to and fro,
To random places. Might it be
That Clarel, who recoil did here,
Shared but that shock of novelty
Which makes some Protestants unglad
First viewing the mysterious cheer
In Peter's fane? Beheld he had,
In Rome beneath the Lateran wall,
The Scala Santa—watched the knees
Of those ascending devotees,
Who, absolution so to reap,
Breathe a low prayer at every step.
Nay, 'twas no novelty at all.
Nor was it that his nature shrunk
But from the curtness of the monk:
Another influence made swerve
And touched him in profounder nerve.
He turned, and passing on enthralled,
Won a still chapel; and one spake
The name. Brief Scripture, here recalled,
The context less obscure may make:
'Tis writ that in a garden's bound
Our Lord was urned. On that green ground
He reappeared, by Mary claimed.
The place, or place alleged, is shown—
Arbors congealed to vaults of stone—
The Apparition's chapel named.
This was the spot where now, in frame
Hard to depict, the student came—
The spot where in the dawning gray,
His pallor with night's tears bedewed,

Restored the Second Adam stood—
Not as in Eden stood the First
All ruddy. Yet, in leaves immersed
And twilight of imperfect day,
Christ seemed the gardener unto her
Misjudging, who in womanhood
Had sought him late in sepulchre
Embowered, nor found.
                Here, votive here—
Here by the shrine that Clarel won—
A wreath shed odors. Scarce that cheer
Warmed some poor Greeks recumbent thrown,
Sore from late journeying far and near,
To hallowed haunts without the town;
So wearied, that no more they kneeled,
But over night here laid them down,
Matrons and children, yet unhealed
Of ache. And each face was a book
Of disappointment. "Why weep'st thou?
Whom seekest?"—words, which chanceful now
Recalled by Clarel, he applied
To these before him; and he took,
In way but little modified,
Part to himself; then stood in dream
Of all which yet might hap to them.
He saw them spent, provided ill—
Pale, huddled in the pilgrim fleet,
Back voyaging now to homes afar.
Midnight, and rising tempests beat—
Such as St. Paul knew—furious war,
To meet which, slender is the skill.
The lamp that burnt upon the prow
In wonted shrine, extinct is now—
Drowned out with Heaven's last feeble star.
Panic ensues; their course is turned;
Toward Tyre they drive—Tyre undiscerned:
A coast of wrecks which warping bleach
On wrecks of piers where eagles screech.
How hopeful from their isles serene
They sailed, and on such tender quest;
Then, after toils that came between,
They re-embarked; and, tho' distressed,
Grieved not, for Zion had been seen;
Each wearing next the heart for charm
Some priestly scrip in leaf of palm.
But these, ah, these in Dawn's pale reign
Asleep upon beach Tyrian!
Or is it sleep? no, rest—that rest

Which naught shall ruffle or molest.
In gliding turn of dreams which mate
He saw from forth Damascus' gate
Tall Islam in her Mahmal go—
Elected camel, king of all,
In mystic housings draped in flow,
Silk fringed, with many a silver ball,
Worked ciphers on the Koran's car
And Sultan's cloth. He hears the jar
Of janizaries armed, a throng
Which drum barbaric, shout and gong
Invest. And camels—robe and shawl
Of riders which they bear along—
Each sheik a pagod on his tower,
Crosslegged and dusky. Therewithal,
In affluence of the opal hour,
Curveting troops of Moslem peers
And flash of scimeters and spears
In groves of grass green pennons fair,
(Like Feiran's palms in fanning air,)
Wherefrom the crescent silvery soars.
Then crowds pell-mell, a concourse wild,
Convergings from Levantine shores;
On foot, on donkeys; litters rare—
Whole families; twin panniers piled;
Rich men and beggars—all beguiled
To cheerful trust in Allah's care;
Allah, toward whose prophet's urn
And Holy City, fond they turn
As forth in pilgrimage they fare.
But long the way. And when they note,
Ere yet they pass wide suburbs green,
Some camp in field, nor far remote,
Inviting, pastoral in scene;
Some child shall leap, and trill in glee
"Mecca, 'tis Mecca, mother—see!"
Then first she thinks upon the waste
Whither the Simoom maketh haste;
Where baskets of the white ribbed dead
Sift the fine sand, while dim ahead
In long, long line, their way to tell,
The bones of camels bleaching dwell,
With skeletons but part interred—
Relics of men which friendless fell;
Whose own hands, in last office, scooped
Over their limbs the sand, but drooped:
Worse than the desert of the Word,
El Tih, the great, the terrible.

Ere town and tomb shall greet the eye
Many shall fall, nor few shall die
Which, punctual at set of sun,
Spread the worn prayer cloth on the sand,
Turning them toward the Mecca stone,
Their shadows ominously thrown
Oblique against the mummy land.
These pass; they fade. What next comes near?
The tawny peasants—human wave
Which rolls over India year by year,
India, the spawning place and grave.
The turbaned billow floods the plains,
Rolling toward Brahma's rarer fanes—
His Compostel or brown Loret
Where sin absolved, may grief forget.
But numbers, plague struck, faint and sore,
Drop livid on the flowery shore—
Arrested, with the locusts sleep,
Or pass to muster where no man may peep.
That vision waned. And, far afloat,
From eras gone he caught the sound
Of hordes from China's furthest moat,
Crossing the Himalayan mound,
To kneel at shrine or relic so
Of Buddha, the Mongolian Fo
Or Indian Saviour. What profound
Impulsion makes these tribes to range?
Stable in time's incessant change
Now first he marks, now awed he heeds
The inter-sympathy of creeds,
Alien or hostile tho' they seem—
Exalted thought or groveling dream.
The worn Greek matrons mark him there:
Ah, young, our lassitude dost share?
Home do thy pilgrim reveries stray?
Art thou too, weary of the way?—
Yes, sympathies of Eve awake;
Yet do but err. For how might break
Upon those simple natures true,
The complex passion? might they view
The apprehension tempest tossed,
The spirit in gulf of dizzying fable lost?

Canto VI - Tribes and Sects

He turned to go; he turned, but stood:

In many notes of varying keys,
From shrines like coves in Jordan's wood
Hark to the rival liturgies,
Which, rolling underneath the dome,
Resound about the patient Tomb
And penetrate the aisles. The rite
Of Georgian and Maronite,
Armenian and fervid Greek,
The Latin organ, and wild clash
Of cymbals smitten cheek to cheek
Which the dark Abyssinian sways;
These like to tides together dash
And question of their purport raise.
If little of the words he knew,
Might Clarel's fancy forge a clue?
A malediction seemed each strain—
Himself the mark: O heart profane,
O pilgrim infidel, begone!
Nor here the sites of Faith pollute,
Thou who misgivest we enthrone
A God untrue, in myth absurd
As monstrous figments blabbed of Jove,
Or, worse, rank lies of Islam's herd:
We know thee, thou there standing mute.
Out, out—begone! try Nature's reign
Who deem'st the supernature vain:
To Lot's Wave by black Kedron rove;
On, by Mount Seir, through Edom move;
There crouch thee with the jackall down—
Crave solace of the scorpion!
'Twas fancy, troubled fancy weaved
Those imputations half believed.
The porch he neared; the chorus swelled;
He went forth like a thing expelled.
Yet, going, he could but recall
The wrangles here which oft befall:
Contentions for each holy place,
And jealousies how far from grace:
O, bickering family bereft,
Was feud the heritage He left?

Canto VII - Beyond the Walls

In street at hand a silence reigns
Which Nature's hush of loneness feigns.
Few casements, few, and latticed deep,

High raised above the head below,
That none might listen, pry, or peep,
Or any hint or inkling know
Of that strange innocence or sin
Which locked itself so close within.
The doors, recessed in massy walls,
And far apart, as dingy were As Bastile gates.
No shape astir Except at whiles a shadow
falls Athwart the way, and key in hand
Noiseless applies it, enters so
And vanishes. By dry airs fanned,
The languid hyssop waveth slow,
Dusty, on stones by ruin rent.
'Twould seem indeed the accomplishment
Whereof the greater prophet tells
In truth's forecasting canticles
Where voice of bridegroom, groom and bride
Is hushed.
Each silent wall and lane—
The city's towers in barren pride
Which still a stifling air detain,
So irked him, with his burden fraught,
Timely the Jaffa Gate he sought,
Thence issued, and at venture went
Along a vague and houseless road
Save narrow houses where abode
The Turk in man's last tenement
Inearthed. But them he heeded not,
Such trance his reveries begot:
"Christ lived a Jew: and in Judea
May linger any breath of Him?
If nay, yet surely it is here
One best may learn if all be dim."
Sudden it came in random play
"Here to Emmaus is the way;"
And Luke's narration straight recurred,
How the two falterers' hearts were stirred
Meeting the Arisen (then unknown)
And listening to his lucid word
As here in place they traveled on.
That scene, in Clarel's temper, bred
A novel sympathy, which said—
I too, I too; could I but meet
Some stranger of a lore replete,
Who, marking how my looks betray
The dumb thoughts clogging here my feet,
Would question me, expound and prove,
And make my heart to burn with love—

Emmaus were no dream today!
He lifts his eyes, and, outlined there,
Saw, as in answer to the prayer,
A man who silent came and slow
Just over the intervening brow
Of a nigh slope. Nearer he drew
Revealed against clear skies of blue;
And—in that Syrian air of charm—
He seemed, illusion such was given,
Emerging from the level heaven,
And vested with its liquid calm.
Scarce aged like time's wrinkled sons,
But touched by chastenings of Eld,
Which halloweth life's simpler ones;
In wasted strength he seemed upheld
Invisibly by faith serene—
Paul's evidence of things not seen.
No staff he carried; but one hand
A solitary Book retained.
Meeting the student's, his mild eyes
Fair greeting gave, in faint surprise.
But, noting that untranquil face,
Concern and anxiousness found place
Beyond the occasion and surmise:
"Young friend in Christ, what thoughts molest
That here ye droop so? Wanderest
Without a guide where guide should be?
Receive one, friend: the book—take ye.
From man to book in startled way
The youth his eyes bent. Book how gray
And weather stained in woeful plight—
Much like that scroll left bare to blight,
Which poet pale, when hope was low,
Bade one who into Libya went,
Fling to the wasteful element,
Yes, leave it there, let wither so.
Ere Clarel ventured on reply
Anew the stranger proffered it,
And in such mode he might espy
It was the page of—Holy Writ.
Then unto him drew Clarel nigher:
"Thou art?" "The sinner Nehemiah."

Canto VIII - The Votary

Sinner?—So spake the saint, a man

Long tarrying in Jewry's court.
With him the faith so well could sort
His home he'd left, nor turned again,
His home by Narraganset's marge,
Giving those years on death which verge
Fondly to that enthusiast part
Oft coming of a stricken heart
Unselfish, which finds solace so.
Though none in sooth might hope to know,
And few surmise his forepast bane,
Such needs have been; since seldom yet
Lone liver was, or wanderer met,
Except he closeted some pain
Or memory thereof. But thence,
May be, was given him deeper sense
Of all that travail life can lend.
Which man may scarce articulate
Better than herds which share.
What end? How hope? turn whither? where was gate
For expectation, save the one
Of beryl, pointed by St. John?
That gate would open, yea, and Christ
Thence issue, come unto His own,
And earth be re-imparadised.
Passages, presages he knew:
Zion restore, convert the Jew,
Reseat him here, the waste bedew;
Then Christ returneth: so it ran.
No founded mission chartered him;
Single in person as in plan,
Absorbed he ranged, in method dim,
A flitting tract dispensing man:
Tracts in each text scribe ever proved
In East which he of Tarsus roved.
Though well such heart might sainthood claim,
Unjust alloy to reverence came.
In Smyrna's mart (sojourning there
Waiting a ship for Joppa's stair)
Pestered he passed thro' Gentile throngs
Teased by an eddying urchin host,
His tracts all fluttering like tongues
The fire flakes of the Pentecost.
Deep read he was in seers devout,
The which forecast Christ's second prime,
And on his slate would cipher out
The mystic days and dates sublime,
And "Time and times and half a time"
Expound he could; and more reveal;

Yet frequent would he feebly steal
Close to one's side, asking, in way
Of weary age—the hour of day.
But how he lived, and what his fare,
Ravens and angels, few beside,
Dreamed or divined. His garments spare
True marvel seemed, nor unallied
To clothes worn by that wandering band
Which ranged and ranged the desert sand
With Moses; and for forty years,
Which two score times re-clad the spheres
In green, and plumed the birds anew,
One vesture wore. From home he brought
The garb which still met sun and dew,
Ashen in shade, by rustics wrought.
Latin, Armenian, Greek, and Jew
Full well the harmless vagrant kenned,
The small meek face, the habit gray:
In him they owned our human clay.
The Turk went further: let him wend;
Him Allah cares for, holy one:
A Santon held him; and was none
Bigot enough scorn's shaft to send.
For, say what cynic will or can,
Man sinless is revered by man
Thro' all the forms which creeds may lend.
And so, secure, nor pointed at,
Among brave Turbans freely roamed the Hat.

Canto IX - Saint and Student

"Nay, take it, friend in Christ," and held
The book in proffer new; the while
His absent eyes of dreamy Eld
Some floating vision did beguile
(Of heaven perchance the wafted hem),
As if in place of earthly wight
A haze of spirits met his sight,
And Clarel were but one of them.
"Consult it, heart; wayfarer you,
And this a friendly guide, the best;
No ground there is that faith would view
But here 'tis rendered with the rest;
The way to fields of Beulah dear
And New Jerusalem is here. "
"I know that guide," said Clarel, "yes;"

And mused awhile in bitterness;
Then turned and studied him again,
Doubting and marveling. A strain
Of trouble seamed the elder brow:
"A pilgrim art thou? pilgrim thou?"
Words simple, which in Clarel bred
More than the simple saint divined;
And, thinking of vocation fled,
Himself he asked: or do I rave,
Or have I left now far behind
The student of the sacred lore?
Direct he then this answer gave:
"I am a traveler—no more."
"Come then with me, in peace we'll go;
These ways of Salem well I know;
Me let be guide whose guide is this,"
And held the Book in witness so,
As 'twere a guide that could not miss:
"Heart, come with me; all times I roam,
Yea, everywhere my work I ply,
In Salem's lanes, or down in gloom
Of narrow glens which outer lie:
Ever I find some passerby.
But thee I'm sent to; share and rove,
With me divide the scrip of love."
Despite the old man's shattered ray,
Won by his mystic saintly way,
Revering too his primal faith,
And grateful for the human claim;
And deeming he must know each path,
And help him so in languid frame
The student gave assent, and caught
Dim solacement to previous thought.

Canto X - Rambles

Days fleet. They rove the storied ground—
Tread many a site that rues the ban
Where serial wrecks on wrecks confound
Era and monument and man;
Or rather, in stratifying way
Bed and impact and overlay.
The Hospitalers' cloisters shamed
Crumble in ruin unreclaimed
On shivered Fatimite palaces
Reared upon crash of Herod's sway—

In turn built on the Maccabees,
And on King David's glory, they;
And David on antiquities
Of Jebusites and Ornan's floor,
And hunters' camps of ages long before.
So Glenroy's tiers of beaches be—
Abandoned margins of the Glacial Sea.
Amid that waste from joy debarred,
How few the islets fresh and green;
Yet on Moriah, tree and sward
In Allah's courts park like were seen
From roof near by; below, fierce ward
Being kept by Mauritanian guard
Of bigot blacks. But of the reign
Of Christ did no memento live
Save soil and ruin? Negative
Seemed yielded in that crumbling fane,
Erst gem to Baldwin's sacred fief,
The chapel of our Dame of Grief.
But hard by Ophel's winding base,
Well watered by the runnel led,
A spot they found, not lacking grace,
Named Garden of King Solomon,
Tho' now a cauliflower bed
To serve the kitchens of the town.
One day as here they came from far,
The saint repeated with low breath.
"Adonijah, Adonijah—
The stumbling stone of Zoheleth."
He wanders, Clarel thought—but no,
For text and chapter did he show
Narrating how the prince in glade,
This very one, the banquet made,
The plotters' banquet, long ago,
Even by the stone named Zoheleth;
But startled by the trump that blew,
Proclaiming Solomon, pale grew
With all his guests.
                    From lower glen
They slanted up the steep, and there
Attained a higher terraced den,
Or small and silent field, quite bare.
The mentor breathed: "Come early here
A sign thou'lt see."— Clarel drew near;
"What sign?" he asked. Whereto with sighs:
"Abashed by morning's holy eyes
This field will crimson, and for shame."
Struck by his fantasy and frame,

Clarel regarded him for time,
Then noted that dull reddish soil,
And caught sight of a thing of grime
Whose aspect made him to recoil—
A rotting charnel house forlorn
Midway inearthed, caved in and torn.
And Clarel knew—one scarce might err—
The field of blood, the bad Aceldama.
By Olivet in waning day
The saint in fond illusion went,
Dream mixed with legend and event;
And as with reminiscence fraught,
Narrated in his rambling way
How here at eve was Christ's resort,
The last low sheep bell tinkling lone—
Christ and the dear disciple—John.
Oft by the Golden Gate that looks
On Shaveh down, and far across
Toward Bethany's secluded nooks—
That gate which sculptures rare emboss
In arches twin; the same where rode
Christ entering with secret load—
Same gate, or on or near the site—
When palms were spread to left and right
Before him, and with sweet acclaim
Were waved by damsels under sway
Of trees where from those branches came—
Over and under palms He went
Unto that crown how different!
The port walled up by Moslem hands
In dread of that predicted day
When pealing hymns, armed Christian bands—
So Islam seers despondent vouch—
Shall storm it, wreathed in Mary's May:
By that sealed gate, in languor's slouch,
How listless in the golden day,
Clarel the mentor frequent heard
The time for Christ's return allot:
A dream, and like a dream it blurred
The sense—faded, and was forgot.
Moved by some mystic impulse, far
From motive known or regular,
The saint would thus his lore unfold,
Though inconclusive; yes, half told
The theme he'd leave, then nod, droop, doze—
Start up and prattle— sigh, and close.

Canto XI - Lower Gihon

Well for the student, might it last,
This dreamful frame which Lethe bred:
Events obtruded, and it passed.
For on a time the twain were led
From Gihon's upper pool and glade
Down to the deeper gulf. They strayed
Along by many silent cells
Cut in the rock, void citadels
Of death. In porch of one was seen
A mat of tender turf, faint green;
And quiet standing on that sward
A stranger whom they overheard
Low murmuring—
"Equivocal! Woo'st thou the weary to thee tell,
Thou tomb, so winsome in thy grace?
To me no reassuring place."
He saw them not; and they, to shun
Disturbing him, passed, and anon
Met three demoniacs, sad three
Ranging those wasteful limits o'er
As in old time. That look they wore
Which in the moody mad bids flee;
'Tis—What have I to do with thee?
Two shunned approach. But one did sit
Lost in some reminiscence sore
Of private wrong outrageous. He,
As at the larger orb of it,
Looming through mists of mind, would bound,
Or cease to pore upon the ground
As late; and so be inly riven
By arrows of indignant pain:
Convulsed in face, he glared at heaven
Then lapsed in sullenness again.
Dire thoughts the pilgrim's mind beset:
"And did Christ come? in such a scene
Encounter the poor Gadarene
Long centuries ago? and yet—
Behold! "
But here came in review—
Though of their nearness unaware—
The stranger, downward wending there,
Who marking Clarel, instant knew—
At least so might his start declare—
A brother that he well might own
In tie of spirit. Young he was,

With crescent forehead—but alas,
Of frame misshaped. Word spake he none,
But vaguely hovered, as may one
Not first who would accost, but deep
Under reserve the wish may keep.
Ere Clarel, here embarrassed grown,
Made recognition, the Unknown
Compressed his lips, turned and was gone.
Mutely for moment, face met face:
But more perchance between the two
Was interchanged than e'en may pass
In many a worded interview.
The student in his heart confessed
A novel sympathy impressed;
And late remissness to retrieve
Fain the encounter would renew.
And yet—if oft one's resolution
Be overruled by constitution—
Herein his heart he might deceive.
Ere long, retracing higher road,
Clarel with Nehemiah stood
By David's Tower, without the wall,
Where black the embattled shadows fall
At morn over Hinnom. Groups were there
Come out to take the evening air,
Watching a young lord Turk in pride,
With fez and sash as red as coral,
And on a steed whose well groomed hide
Was all one burnished burning sorrel,
Scale the lit slope; then veering wide,
Rush down into the gloomful gorge,
The steel hoof showering sparks as from a forge.
Even Nehemiah, in senile tone
Of dreamy interest, was won
That shooting star to gaze upon.
But rallying, he bent his glance
Toward the opposing eminence;
And turning, "Seest thou not," he said,
"As sinks the sun beyond this glen
Of Moloch. how clouds intervene
And hood the brightness that was shed?
But yet few hours and he will rise
In better place, and beauty get;
Yea, friend in Christ, in morning skies
Return he will over Olivet:
And we shall greet him. Say ye so?
Betimes then will we up and go.
Farewell. At early dawn await

Christ's bondman old at Stephen's Gate."

Canto XII - Celio

But ere they meet in place assigned,
It needs—to make the sequel clear—
A crossing thread be first entwined.
Within the Terra-Santa's wall
(A prefix dropped, the Latins here
So the Franciscan Convent call),
Commended to the warden's care,
The mitred father-warden there,
By missives from a cardinal,
It chanced an uncompanioned youth.
By birth a Roman, shelter found.
In casual contact, daily round,
Mixed interest the stranger won.
Each friar, the humblest, could but own
His punctual courtesy, in sooth,
Though this still guarded a reserve
Which, not offending, part estranged.
Sites, sites and places all he ranged
Unwearied, but would ever swerve
From escort such as here finds place,
Or cord-girt guide, or chamberlain
Martial in Oriental town,
By gilt-globed staff of office known,
Sword by his side, in golden lace,
Tall herald making clear the van.

But what most irked each tonsured man,
Distrust begat, concern of heart,
Was this: though the young man took part
In chapel service, 'twas as guest
Who but conformed; he showed no zest
Of faith within, faith personal.
Ere long the warden, kindly all,
Said inly with himself: Poor boy,
Enough hast thou of life-annoy;
Let be reproach. Tied up in knot
Of body by the fleshly withes,
Needs must it be the spirit writhes
And takes a warp. But Christ will blot
Some records in the end.
And own,
So far as in by out is shown,

Not idle was the monk's conceit.
Fair head was set on crook and lump,
Absalom's locks but Esop's hump.
Deep in the grave eyes' last retreat,
One read thro' guarding feint of pride,
Quick sense of all the ills that gride
In one contorted so. But here,
More to disclose in bearing chief,
More than to monks might well appear,
There needs some running mention brief.

Fain had his brethren have him grace
Some civic honorable place;
And interest was theirs to win
Ample preferment; he as kin
Was loved, if but ill understood:
At heart they had his worldly good;
But he postponed, and went his way
Unpledged, unhampered. So that still
Leading a studious life at will,
And prompted by an earnest mind,
Scarce might he shun the fevered sway
Of focused question in our day.
Overmuch he shared, but in that kind

Which marks the Italian turn of thought,
When, counting Rome's tradition naught,
The mind is coy to own the rule
Of sect replacing, sect or school.
At sea, in brig which swings no boat,
To founder is to sink.
On day
When from St. Peter's balcony,
The raised pontific fingers bless
The city and the world; the stress
He knew of fate: Blessest thou me,
One wave here in this heaving sea
Of heads? how may a blessing be?
Luckless, from action's thrill removed,
And all that yields our nature room;
In courts a jest; and, harder doom,
Never the hunchback may be loved.
Never! for Beatrice—Bice—O,
Diminutive once sweet, made now
All otherwise!—didst thou but fool?
Arch practice in precocious school?
Nay, rather 'twas ere thou didst bud
Into thy riper womanhood.

Since love, arms, courts, abjure why then
Remaineth to me what? the pen?
Dead feather of ethereal life!
Nor efficacious much, save when
It makes some fallacy more rife.
My kin—I blame them not at heart—
Would have me act some routine part,
Subserving family, and dreams
Alien to me illusive schemes.
This world clean fails me: still I yearn.
Me then it surely does concern
Some other world to find. But where?
In creed? I do not find it there.
That said, and is the emprise o'er?
Negation, is there nothing more?
This side the dark and hollow bound

Lies there no unexplored rich ground?
Some other world: well, there's the New—
Ah, joyless and ironic too!
They vouch that virgin sphere's assigned
Seat for man's re-created kind:
Last hope and proffer, they protest.
Brave things! sun rising in the west;
And bearded centuries but gone
For ushers to the beardless one.
Nay, nay; your future's too sublime:
The Past, the Past is half of time,
The proven half.—Thou Pantheon old,
Two thousand years have round thee rolled:
Yet thou, in Rome, thou bid'st me seek
Wisdom in something more antique
Than thou thyself. Turn then: what seer,
The senior of this Latian one,
Speaks from the ground, transported here
In Eastern soil? Far buried down—
For consecration and a grace
Enlocking Santa Croce's base—
Lies earth of Jewry, which of yore
The homeward bound Crusaders bore
In fleet from Jaffa.—Trajan's hall,
That huge ellipse imperial,
Was built by Jews. And Titus' Arch

Transmits their conqueror in march
Of trophies which those piers adorn.
There yet, for an historic plea,
In heathen triumph's harlotry

The Seven-Branched Candlestick is borne.
What then? Tho' all be whim of mine,
Yet by these monuments I'm schooled,
Arrested, strangely overruled;
Methinks I catch a beckoning sign,
A summons as from Palestine.
Yea, let me view that pontiff-land
Whose sway occult can so command;
Make even Papal Rome to be

Her appanage or her colony.
Is Judah's mummy quite unrolled?
To pluck the talisman from fold!
But who may well indeed forecast
The novel influence of scenes
Remote from his habitual Past?
The unexpected supervenes;
Which Celio proved. 'Neath Zion's lee
His nature, with that nature blent,
Evoked an upstart element,
As do the acid and the alkali

Canto XIII - The Arch

Blue-lights sent up by ship forlorn
Are answered oft but by the glare
Of rockets from another, torn
In the same gale's inclusive snare.

'Twas then when Celio was lanced
By novel doubt, the encounter chanced
In Gihon, as recited late,
And at a time when Clarel too,
On his part, felt the grievous weight
Of those demoniacs in view;
So that when Celio advanced
No wonder that the meeting eyes
Betrayed reciprocal surmise
And interest. 'Twas thereupon
The Italian, as the eve drew on,
Regained the gate, and hurried in
As he would passionately win
Surcease to thought by rapid pace.
Eastward he bent, across the town,
Till in the Via Crucis lone
An object there arrested him.

With gallery which years deface,
Its bulk athwart the alley grim,

The arch named Ecce Homo threw;
The same, if child-like faith be true,
From which the Lamb of God was shown
By Pilate to the wolfish crew.
And Celio—in frame how prone
To kindle at that scene recalled—
Perturbed he stood, and heart-enthralled.
No raptures which with saints prevail,
Nor trouble of compunction born
He felt, as there he seemed to scan
Aloft in spectral guise, the pale
Still face, the purple robe, and thorn;
And inly cried—Behold the Man!
Yon Man it is this burden lays:
Even he who in the pastoral hours,
Abroad in fields, and cheered by flowers,
Announced a heaven's unclouded days;
And, ah, with such persuasive lips—
Those lips now sealed while doom delays—
Won men to look for solace there;
But, crying out in death's eclipse,
When rainbow none his eyes might see,
Enlarged the margin for despair—
My God, my God, forsakest me?
Upbraider! we upbraid again;
Thee we upbraid; our pangs constrain

Pathos itself to cruelty.
Ere yet thy day no pledge was given
Of homes and mansions in the heaven—
Paternal homes reserved for us;
Heart hoped it not, but lived content—
Content with life's own discontent,
Nor deemed that fate ere swerved for us:
The natural law men let prevail;
Then reason disallowed the state
Of instinct's variance with fate.
But thou—ah, see, in rack how pale
Who did the world with throes convulse;
Behold him—yea—behold the Man

Who warranted if not began
The dream that drags out its repulse.
Nor less some cannot break from thee;
Thy love so locked is with thy lore,

They may not rend them and go free:
The head rejects; so much the more
The heart embraces—what? the love?
If true what priests avouch of thee,
The shark thou mad'st, yet claim'st the dove.
Nature and thee in vain we search:
Well urged the Jews within the porch—
"How long wilt make us still to doubt?"
How long?—'Tis eighteen cycles now—
Enigma and evasion grow;
And shall we never find thee out?
What isolation lones thy state
That all we else know cannot mate
With what thou teachest? Nearing thee
All footing fails us; history
Shows there a gulf where bridge is none!
In lapse of unrecorded time,
Just after the apostles' prime,
What chance or craft might break it down?
Served this a purpose? By what art
Of conjuration might the heart
Of heavenly love, so sweet, so good,
Corrupt into the creeds malign,
Begetting strife's pernicious brood,
Which claimed for patron thee divine?
Anew, anew,
For this thou bleedest, Anguished Face;
Yea, thou through ages to accrue,
Shalt the Medusa shield replace:
In beauty and in terror too
Shalt paralyze the nobler race—
Smite or suspend, perplex, deter—
Tortured, shalt prove a torturer.
Whatever ribald Future be,

Thee shall these heed, amaze their hearts with thee
Thy white, thy red, thy fairness and thy tragedy.

He turned, uptorn in inmost frame,
Nor weened he went the way he came,
Till meeting two there, nor in calm—
A monk and layman, one in creed,
The last with novice-ardor warm,
New-comer, and devout indeed,
To whom the other was the guide,
And showed the Places. "Here," he cried,
At pause before a wayside stone,
"Thou mark'st the spot where that bad Jew

His churlish taunt at Jesus threw
Bowed under cross with stifled moan:
Caitiff, which for that cruel wrong
Thenceforth till Doomsday drives along."
Starting, as here he made review,
Celio winced—Am I the Jew?
Without delay, afresh he turns
Descending by the Way of Thorns,
Winning the Proto-Martyr's gate,
And goes out down Jehoshaphat.
Beside him slid the shadows flung
By evening from the tomb-stones tall
Upon the bank far sloping from the wall.
Scarce did he heed, or did but slight
The admonishment the warder rung
That with the setting of the sun,
Now getting low and all but run,
The gate would close, and for the night.

Canto XIV - In the Glen

If Savonarola's zeal devout
But with the fagot's flame died out;
If Leopardi, stoned by Grief,
A young St. Stephen of the Doubt,
Might merit well the martyr's leaf;
In these if passion held her claim,
Let Celio pass, of breed the same,
Nor ask from him—not found in them—
The Attic calm, or Saxon phlegm.
Night glooming now in valley dead,
The Italian turned, regained the gate,
But found it closed, the warder fled,
And strange hush of an Eastern town
Where life retreats with set of sun.
Before the riveted clamped wood
Alone in outer dark he stood.
A symbol is it? be it so:
Harbor remains, I'll thither go.
A point there is where Kedron's shore
Narrowing, deepening, steepening more,
Shrinks to an adamantine pass
Flanked by three tombs, from base to head
Hewn from the cliff in cubic mass,
One quite cut off and islanded,
And one presents in Petra row

Pillars in hanging portico
Or balcony, here looking down
Vacantly on the vacant glen:
A place how dead, hard by a town.
'Twas here that Celio made his den
Where erst, as by tradition held,
St. James from hunters lay concealed,
Levites and bigots of the thong.
Hour after hour slow dragged along.
The glen's wall with night roundabout
Blended as cloud with cloud-rack may.
But lo—as when off Tamura
The splash of north-lights on the sea
Crimsons the bergs—so here start out
Some crags aloft how vividly.
Apace he won less narrow bound.
From the high gate, behold, a stream

Of torches. Lava-like it wound
Out from the city locked in dream,
And red adown the valley flowed.
Was it his friends the friars? from height
Meet rescue bringing in that light
To one benighted? Yes, they showed
A file of monks. But—how? their wicks
Invest a shrouded crucifix;
And each with flambeau held in hand,
Craped laymen mingle with the band
Of cord-girt gowns. He looks again:
Yes, 'tis the Terra Santa's train.
Nearer they come. The warden goes,
And other faces Celio knows.
Upon an office these are bound
Consolatory, which may stem
The affliction, or relieve the wound
Of those which mute accompany them
In mourners' garb.
Aside he shrunk
Until had passed the rearmost monk;
Then, cloaked, he followed them in glade
Where fell the shadow deeper made.
Kedron they cross. Much so might move—

If legend hold, which none may prove,—
The remnant of the Twelve which bore
Down thro' this glen in funeral plight
The Mother of our Lord by night
To sepulcher. Nay, just before

Her tomb alleged, the monks and they
Which mourn, pause and uplift a lay;
Then rise, pass on, and bow the knee
In dust beside Gethsemane.
One named the Bitter Cup, and said:
"Saviour, thou knowest: it was here
The angels ministered, thy head
Supported, kissed thy lidded eyes
And pale swooned cheek till thou didst rise;
Help these then, unto these come near!"

Out sobbed the mourners, and the tear
From Celio trickled; but he mused—
Weak am I, by a myth abused.
Up Olivet the torch-light train
Filed slowly, yielding tribute-strain
At every sacred place they won;
Nor tarried long, but journeyed on
To Bethany—thro' stony lane
Went down into the narrow house
Or void cave named from Lazarus.
The flambeaux redden the dark wall,
Their shadows on that redness fall.
To make the attestation rife,
The resurrection and the life
Through Him the lord of miracle
The warden from the page doth bruit
The story of the man that died
And lived again—bound hand and foot
With grave-clothes, rose—electrified;
Whom then they loosed, let go; even he
Whom many people came to see,
The village hinds and farm-house maids,
Afterward, at the supper given
To Jesus in the balmy even,
Who raised him vital from the shades.
The lesson over, well they sang
"O death, where is thy sting? O grave,
Where is thy victory?" It rang,
And ceased. And from the outward cave
These tones were heard: "But died he twice?
He comes not back from Paradise
Or Hades now. A vacant tomb
By Golgotha they show—a cell,
A void cell here. And is it well?
Raiser and raised divide one doom;
Both vanished now."
No thrills forewarn

Of fish that leaps from midnight tarn;
The very wave from which it springs

Is startled and recoils in rings.
So here with Celio and the word
Which from his own rash lips he heard.
He, hastening forth now all unseen,
Recrossed the mountain and ravine,
Nor paused till on a mound he sate
Biding St. Stephen's opening gate.
Ere long in gently fanning flaws
An odoriferous balmy air
Foreruns the morning, then withdraws,
Or—westward heralding—roves there.
The startled East a tremor knows—
Flushes—anon superb appears
In state of housings, shawls and spears,
Such as the Sultan's vanguard shows.
Preceded thus, in pomp the sun
August from Persia draweth on,
Waited by groups upon the wall
Of Judah's upland capital.

Canto XV - Under the Minaret

"Lo, shoot the spikes above the hill:
Now expectation grows and grows;
Yet vain the pageant, idle still:

When one would get at Nature's will—
To be put off by purfled shows!
"He breaks. Behold, thou orb supreme,
'Tis Olivet which thou ascendest—
The hill and legendary chapel;
Yet how indifferent thy beam!
Awe nor reverence pretendest:
Dome and summit dost but dapple
With gliding touch, a tinging gleam:
Knowest thou the Christ? believest in the dream?"
'Twas Celio—seated there, as late,
Upon the mound. But now the gate,
Flung open, welcomes in the day,

And lets out Clarel with the guide;
These from the wall had hailed the ray;
And Celio heard them there aside,

And turning, rose. Was it to greet?
But ere they might accost or meet,
From minaret in grounds hard by
Of Omar, the muezzin's cry—
Tardy, for Mustapha was old,
And age a laggard is—was rolled,
Announcing Islam's early hour
Of orison. Along the walls
And that deep gulf over which these tower—
Far down toward Rogel, hark, it calls!
Can Siloa hear it, yet her wave
So listless lap the hollow cave?
Is Zion deaf? But, promptly still,
Each turban at that summons shrill,
Which should have called ere perfect light,
Bowed—hands on chest, or arms upright;
While over all those fields of loss
Where now the Crescent rides the Cross,
Sole at the marble mast-head stands
The Islam herald, his two hands
Upon the rail, and sightless eyes
Turned upward reverent toward the skies.
And none who share not this defect
The rules to function here elect;
Since, raised upon the lifted perch
What leave for prying eyes to search
Into the privacies that lurk
In courts domestic of the Turk,
Whose tenements in every town
Guard well against the street alone.
But what's evoked in Clarel's mien—
What look, responsive look is seen
In Celio, as together there
They pause? Can these a climax share?
Mutual in approach may glide
Minds which from poles adverse have come,
Belief and unbelief? may doom
Of doubt make such to coincide—
Upon one frontier brought to dwell
Arrested by the Ezan high
In summons as from out the sky
To matins of the infidel?
The God alleged, here in abode
Ignored with such impunity,
Scarce true is writ a jealous God.
Think ye such thoughts? If so it be,
Yet these may eyes transmit and give?
Mere eyes? so quick, so sensitive?

Howbeit Celio knew his mate:
Again, as down in Gihon late,
He hovered with his overture—
An overture that scorned debate.
But inexperienced, shy, unsure—
Challenged abrupt, or yea or nay,
Again did Clarel hesitate;
When quick the proud one with a look
Which might recoil of heart betray,
And which the other scarce might brook
In recollection, turned away.
Ah, student, ill thy sort have sped:
The instant proffer—it is fled!
When, some days after, for redress
Repentant Clarel sought access,

He learned the name, with this alone—
From convent Celio was gone,
Nor knew they whither.
Here in press
To Clarel came a dreamy token:
What speck is that so far away
That wanes and wanes in waxing day?
Is it the sail ye fain had spoken
Last night when surges parted ye?
But on, it is a boundless sea.

XVI - The Wall of Wail

Beneath the toppled ruins old
In series from Moriah rolled
Slips Kedron furtive? underground
Peasants avouch they hear the sound.
In aisled lagunes and watery halls
Under the temple, silent sleep
What memories elder? Far and deep
What ducts and chambered wells and walls
And many deep substructions be
Which so with doubt and gloom agree,
To question one is borne along—
Based these the Right? subserved the Wrong?
'Twas by an all-forgotten way,
Whose mouth in outer glen forbid
By heaps of rubbish long lay hid,
Cloaca of remotest day;
'Twas by that unsuspected vault

With outlet in mid city lone,
A spot with ruin all bestrown—
The peasants in sedition late
Captured Jerusalem in strait,
Took it by underground assault.
Go wander, and within the walls,
Among the glades of cactus trees
Where no life harbors, peers or calls—
Wild solitudes like shoals in seas
Unsailed; or list at still sundown,
List to the hand-mills as they drone,
Domestic hand-mills in the court,
And groups there in the dear resort,
Mild matron pensive by her son,
The little prattler at her knee:
Under such scenes abysses be—
Dark quarries where few care to pry,
Whence came those many cities high—
Great capitals successive reared,
And which successive disappeared

On this same site. To powder ground,
Dispersed their dust blows round and round.
No shallow gloss may much avail
When these or kindred thoughts assail:
Which Clarel proved, the more he went
A rover in their element.
For—trusting still that in some place
Where pilgrims linger he anew
The missing stranger yet would face
And speak with—never he withdrew
His wandering feet.
In aimless sort
Passing across the town amort,
They came where, camped in corner waste,
Some Edomites were at repast—
Sojourners mere, and of a day—
Dark-hued, nor unlike birds of prey
Which on the stones of Tyre alight.
While Clarel fed upon that sight—
The saint repeating in his ear
Meet text applying to the scene—
As liberated from ravine,
Voices in choral note they hear;
And, strange as lilies in morass,
At the same moment, lo, appear
Emerging from a stony pass,

A lane low-vaulted and unclean,
Damsels in linen robes, heads bare,
Enlinked with matrons pacing there,
And elders gray; the maids with book:
Companions would one page o'erlook;
And vocal thus they wound along,
No glad procession, spite the song.
For truth to own, so downcast they—
At least the men, in sordid dress
And double file—the slim array,
But for the maidens' gentleness
And voices which so bird-like sang,
Had seemed much like a coffle gang.

But Nehemiah a key supplied:
"Alas, poor misled Jews," he sighed,
"Ye do but dirge among your dead.—
The Hebrew quarter here we tread;
And this is Friday; Wailing Day:
These to the temple wend their way.
And shall we follow?" Doing so
They came upon a sunken yard
Obscure, where dust and rubbish blow.
Felonious place, and quite debarred
From common travel. On one side
A blind wall rose, stable and great—
Massed up immense, an Ararat
Founded on beveled blocks how wide,
Reputed each a stone august
Of Solomon's fane (else fallen to dust)
But now adopted for the wall
To Islam's courts. There, lord of all,
The Turk permits the tribes to creep
Abject in rear of those dumb stones,
To lean or kneel, lament and weep;
Sad mendicants shut out from gate
Inexorable. Sighs and groans:
To be restored! we wait, long wait!
They call to count their pristine state
On this same ground: the lifted rows
Of peristyles; the porticoes
Crown upon crown, where Levite trains
In chimes of many a silver bell
(Daintily small as pearls in chain)
Hemming their mantles musical—
Passed in procession up and down,
Viewing the belt of guarding heights,
And march of shadows there, and flights

Of pigeon-pets, and palm leaves blown;
Or heard the silver trumpets call—
The priestly trumps, to festival.
So happy they; such Judah's prime.
But we, the remnant, lo, we pale;

Cast from the Temple, here we wail—
Yea, perish ere come Shiloh's time.
Hard by that joyless crew which leant
With brows against the adamant—
Sad buttresses thereto—hard by—
The student marks the Black Jew bowed;
His voice he hears amid the crowd
Which supplicate stern Shaddai.
And earnest, too, he seeth there
One scarcely Hebrew in his dress
Rural, and hard cheek's swarthiness,
With nothing of an Eastern air.
His eyes met Clarel's unremoved—
In end a countryman he proved,
A strange apostate. On the twain
Contrasted so—the white, the black—
Man's earliest breed and latest strain—
Behind the master Moslem's back
Skulking, and in great Moses' track—
Gazed Clarel with the wonderment
Of wight who feels the earth upheave
Beneath him, and learns, ill-content,
That terra firma can deceive.
When now those Friday wails were done,
Nehemiah, sidling with his book
Unto a lorn decrepit one,

Proferred a tract: "'Tis Hebrew, look,"
Zealous he urged; "it points the way,
Sole way, dear heart, whereby ye may
Rebuild the Temple." Answer none
Gat he from Isaac's pauper son,
Who, turning, part as in disdain,
Crept toward his squalid home. Again
Enrapt stood Clarel, lost awhile:
"Yon Jew has faith; can faith be vain?
But is it faith? ay, faith 's the word—
What else? Faith then can thus beguile
Her faithfulest. Hard, that is hard!"
So doubts invaded. found him out.

He strove with them; but they proved stout,

Nor would they down.
But turn regard.
Among the maids those rites detained,
One he perceived, as it befell,
Whose air expressed such truth unfeigned,
And harmonies inlinked which dwell
In pledges born of record pure—
She looked a legate to insure
That Paradise is possible
Now as hereafter. 'Twas the grace
Of Nature's dawn: an Eve-like face
And Nereid eyes with virgin spell
Candid as day, yet baffling quite
Like day, through unreserve of light.
A dove she seemed, a temple dove,
Born in the temple or its grove,
And nurtured there. But deeper viewed,
What was it that looked part amiss?
A bit impaired? what lack of peace?
Enforced suppression of a mood,
Regret with yearning intertwined,
And secret protest of a virgin mind.
Hebrew the profile, every line;
But as in haven fringed with palm,
Which Indian reefs embay from harm,
Belulled as in the vase the wine—
Red budded corals in remove,
Peep coy through quietudes above;
So through clear olive of the skin,
And features finely Hagarene;
Its way a tell-tale flush did win—
A tint which unto Israel's sand
Blabbed of the June in some far clover land.
Anon by chance the damsel's eye
Fell on Nehemiah, and the look
A friendly recognition spoke,
Returned in kind. When by-and-by
The groups brake up and homeward bent;

Then, nor unnoted by the youth,
That maiden with the apostate went,
Whose voice paternal called her—"Ruth!"
"Tell, friend," said Clarel eagerly,
As from the wall of wail they passed;
"Father and daughter? Who may be
That strange pervert?" No willing haste
The mentor showed; awhile he fed
On anxious thoughts; then grievingly

The story gave—a tangled thread,
Which, cleared from snarl and ordered so,
Follows transferred, with interflow
Of much Nehemiah scarce might add.

Canto XXVII - Nathan

Nathan had sprung from worthy stock—
Austere, ascetical, but free,
Which hewed their way from sea-beat rock
Wherever woods and winter be.
The pilgrim-keel in storm and stress
Had erred, and on a wilderness.
But shall the children all be schooled
By hap which their forefathers ruled?
Those primal settlers put in train

New emigrants which inland bore;
From these too, emigrants again
Westward pressed further; more bred more;
At each remove a goodlier wain,
A heart more large, an ampler shore,
With legacies of farms behind;
Until in years the wagons wind
Through parks and pastures of the sun,
Warm plains as of Esdraleon:
'Tis nature in her best benign.
Wild, wild in symmetry of mould
With freckles on her tawny gold,
The lily alone looks pantherine—

The libbard-lily. Never broods
The gloom here of grim hemlock woods
Breeding the witcheraft-spell malign;
But groves like isles in Grecian seas,
Those dotting isles, the Sporades.
But who the gracious charm may tell—
Long rollings of the vast serene—
The prairie in her swimming swell
Of undulation.
Such glad scene
Was won by venturers from far
Born under that severer star
The landing patriarchs knew. In fine,
To Illinois—a turf divine
Of promise, how auspicious spread,

Ere yet the cities rose thereon—
From Saco's mountain wilds were led
The sire of Nathan, wife and son;
Life's lot to temper so, and shun
Mountains whose camp withdrawn was set
Above one vale he would forget.
After some years their tale had told,
He rested; lay forever stilled
With sachems and mound-builders old.
The son was grown; the farm he tilled;
A stripling, but of manful ways,
Hardy and frugal, oft he filled
The widow's eyes with tears of praise.
An only child, with her he kept
For her sake part, the Christian way,
Though frequent in his bosom crept
Precocious doubt unbid. The sway
He felt of his grave life, and power
Of vast space, from the log-house door
Daily beheld. Thrce Indian mounds
Against the horizon's level bounds
Dim showed across the prairie green
Like dwarfed and blunted mimic shapes
Of Pyramids at distance seen

From the broad Delta's planted capes
Of vernal grain. In nearer view
With trees he saw them crowned, which drew
From the red sagamores of eld
Entombed within, the vital gum
Which green kept each mausoleum.
Hard by, as chanced, he once beheld
Bones like sea corals; one bleached skull
A vase vined round and beautiful
With flowers; felt, with bated breath
The floral revelry over death.
And other sights his heart had thrilled;
Lambs had he known by thunder killed,
Innocents—and the type of Christ
Betrayed. Had not such things sufficed
To touch the young pure heart with awe,
Memory's mint could move him more.
In prairie twilight, summer's own,
The last cow milked, and he alone
In barn-yard dreamy by the fence,
Contrasted, came a scene immense:
The great White Hills, mount flanked by mount,
The Saco and Ammonoosuc's fount;

Where, in September's equinox
Nature hath put such terror on
That from his mother man would run—

Our mother, Earth: the founded rocks
Unstable prove: the Slide! the Slide!
Again he saw the mountain side
Sliced open; yet again he stood
Under its shadow, on the spot—
Now waste, but once a cultured plot,
Though far from village neighborhood—
Where, nor by sexton hearsed at even,
Somewhere his uncle slept; no mound,
Since not a trace of him was found,
So whelmed the havoc from the heaven.
This reminiscence of dismay,
These thoughts unhinged him. On a day

Waiting for monthly grist at mill
In settlement some miles away,
It chanced, upon the window-sill
A dusty book he spied, whose coat,
Like the Scotch miller's powdered twill,
The mealy owner might denote.
Called off from reading, unaware
The miller e'en had left it there.
A book all but forsaken now
For more advanced ones not so frank,
Nor less in vogue and taking rank;
And yet it never shall outgrow
That infamy it first incurred,
Though—viewed in light which moderns know—
Capricious infamy absurd.
The blunt straightforward Saxon tone,
Work-a-day language, even his own,
The sturdy thought, not deep but clear,
The hearty unbelief sincere,
Arrested him much like a hand
Clapped on the shoulder. Here he found
Body to doubt, rough standing-ground.
After some pages brief were scanned,
"Wilt loan me this?" he anxious said.
The shrewd Scot turned his square, strong head—
The book he saw, in troubled trim,
Fearing for Nathan, even him
So young, and for the mill, may be,
Should his unspoken heresy
Get bruited so. The lad but part

Might penetrate that senior heart.
Vainly the miller would dissuade;
Pledge gave he, and the loan was made.
Reclined that night by candle dim
He read, then slept, and woke afraid:
The White Hill's slide! the Indian skull!
But this wore off; and unto him
Came acquiescence, which tho' dull
Was hardly peace. An altered earth

Sullen he tilled, in Adam's frame
When thrust from Eden out to dearth
And blest no more, and wise in shame.
The fall! nor aught availed at need
To Nathan, not each filial deed
Done for his mother, to allay
This ill. But tho' the Deist's sway,
Broad as the prairie fire, consumed
Some pansies which before had bloomed
Within his heart; it did but feed
To clear the soil for upstart weed.
Yes, ere long came replacing mood.
The god, expelled from given form,
Went out into the calm and storm.
Now, ploughing near the isles of wood
In dream he felt the loneness come,
In dream regarded there the loam
Turned first by him. Such mental food
Need quicken, and in natural way,
Each germ of Pantheistic sway,
Whose influence, nor always drear,
Tenants our maiden hemisphere;
As if, dislodged long since from cells
Of Thracian woodlands, hither stole
Hither, to renew their old control—
Pan and the pagan oracles.

How frequent when Favonius low
Breathed from the copse which mild did wave
Over his father's sylvan grave,
And stirred the corn, he stayed the hoe,
And leaning, listening, felt a thrill
Which heathenized against the will.

Years sped. But years attain not truth,
Nor length of life avails at all;
But time instead contributes ruth:
His mother—her the garners call:

When sicklemen with sickles go,
The churl of nature reaps her low.

Let now the breasts of Ceres swell—
In shooks, with golden tassels gay,
The Indian corn its trophies ray
About the log-house; is it well
With death's ripe harvest?—To believe,
Belief to win nor more to grieve!
But how? a sect about him stood
In thin and scattered neighborhood;
Uncanny, and in rupture new;
Nor were all lives of members true
And good. For them who hate and heave
Contempt on rite and creed sublime,
Yet to their own rank fable cleave—
Abject, the latest shame of time;
These quite repelled, for still his mind
Erring, was of no vulgar kind.
Alone, and at Doubt's freezing pole
He wrestled with the pristine forms
Like the first man. By inner storms
Held in solution, so his soul
Ripened for hour of such control
As shapes, concretes. The influence came,
And from a source that well might claim
Surpnse.
          'Twas in a lake-port new,
A mart for grain, by chance he met
A Jewess who about him threw
Else than Nerea's amorous net
And dubious wile. 'Twas Miriam's race:
A sibyl breathed in Agar's grace—
A sibyl, but a woman too;
He felt her grateful as the rains
To Rephaim and the Rama plains
In drought. Ere won, herself did woo:
"Wilt join my people?" Love is power;
Came the strange plea in yielding hour.
Nay, and turn Hebrew? But why not?
If backward still the inquirer goes
To get behind man's present lot

Of crumbling faith; for rear-ward shows
Far behind Rome and Luther what?
The crag of Sinai. Here then plant
Thyself secure: 'tis adamant.
Still as she dwelt on Zion's story

He felt the glamour, caught the gleam;
All things but these seemed transitory—
Love, and his love's Jerusalem.
And interest in a mitred race,
With awe which to the fame belongs,
These in receptive heart found place
When Agar chanted David's songs.
'Twas passion. But the Puritan—
Mixed latent in his blood—a strain
How evident, of Hebrew source;
'Twas that, diverted here in force,
Which biased—hardly might do less.
Hereto append, how earnestness,
Which disbelief for first-fruits bore,
Now, in recoil, by natural stress
Constrained to faith—to faith in more
Than prior disbelief had spurned;
As if, when he toward credence turned,
Distance therefrom but gave career
For impetus that shot him sheer
Beyond. Agar rejoiced; nor knew

How such a nature, charged with zeal,
Might yet overpass that limit due
Observed by her. For woe or weal
They wedded, one in heart and creed.
Transferring fields with title-deed,
From rustic life he quite withdrew—
Traded, and throve. Two children came:
Sedate his heart, nor sad the dame.
But years subyert; or he outgrew
(While yet confirmed in all the myth)
The mind infertile of the Jew.
His northern nature, full of pith
Vigor and enterprise and will,

Having taken thus the Hebrew bent,
Might not abide inactive so
And but the empty forms fulfill:
Needs utilize the mystic glow—
For nervous energies find vent.
The Hebrew seers announce in time
The return of Judah to her prime;
Some Christians deemed it then at hand.
Here was an object: Up and do!
With seed and tillage help renew—
Help reinstate the Holy Land.
Some zealous Jews on alien soil

Who still from Gentile ways recoil,
And loyally maintain the dream,
Salute upon the Paschal day
With Next year in Jerusalem!
Now Nathan turning unto her,
Greeting his wife at morning ray,
Those words breathed on the Passover;
But she, who mutely startled lay,
In the old phrase found import new,
In the blithe tone a bitter cheer
That did the very speech subdue.
She kenned her husband's mind austere,
Had watched his reveries grave; he meant
No flourish mere of sentiment.
Then what to do? or how to stay?
Decry it? that would faith unsay.
Withstand him? but she gently loved.
And so with Agar here it proved,
As oft it may, the hardy will
Overpowered the deep monition still.

Enough; fair fields and household charms
They quit, sell all, and cross the main
With Ruth and a young child in arms.
A tract secured on Sharon's plain,
Some sheds he built, and 'round walled in
Defensive; toil severe but vain.
The wandering Arabs, wonted long
(Nor crime they deemed it, crime nor sin)
To scale the desert convents strong—
In sly foray leaped Nathan's fence
And robbed him; and no recompense
Attainable where law was none
Or perjured. Resolute hereon,
Agar, with Ruth and the young child,
He lodged within the stronghold town
Of Zion, and his heart exiled
To abide the worst on Sharon's lea.
Himself and honest servants three
Armed husbandmen became, as erst
His sires in Pequod wilds immersed.
Hittites—foes pestilent to God
His fathers old those Indians deemed:
Nathan the Arabs here esteemed
The same—slaves meriting the rod;
And out he spake it; which bred hate
The more imperiling his state.
With muskets now his servants slept;

Alternate watch and ward they kept
In grounds beleaguered. Not the less
Visits at stated times he made
To them in Zion's walled recess.
Agar with sobs of suppliance prayed

That he would fix there: "Ah, for good
Tarry! abide with us, thine own;
Put not these blanks between us; should
Such space be for a shadow thrown?
Quit Sharon, husband; leave to brood;
Serve God by cleaving to thy wife,
Thy children. If come fatal strife—
Which I forebode—nay!" and she flung
Her arms about him there, and clung.
She plead. But tho' his heart could feel,
'Twas mastered by inveterate zeal.

Even the nursling's death ere long
Balked not his purpose tho' it wrung.

But Time the cruel, whose smooth way
Is feline, patient for the prey
That to this twig of being clings;
And Fate, which from her ambush springs
And drags the loiterer soon or late
Unto a sequel unforeseen;
These doomed him and cut short his date;
But first was modified the lien
The husband had on Agar's heart;
And next a prudence slid athwart—
After distrust. But be unsaid
That steep toward which the current led.
Events shall speak.
And now the guide,
Who did in sketch this tale begin,
Parted with Clarel at the inn;
And ere long came the eventide.

Canto XVIII - Night

Like sails convened when calms delay
Off the twin forelands on fair day,
So, on Damascus' plain behold
Mid groves and gardens, girdling ones,
White fleets of sprinkled villas, rolled

In the green ocean of her environs.
There when no minaret receives
The sun that gilds yet St. Sophia,
Which loath and later it bereaves,
The peace fulfills the heart's desire.
In orchards mellowed by eve's ray
The prophet's son in turban green,
Mild, with a patriarchal mien,
Gathers his fruity spoil. In play
Of hide-and-seek where alleys be,

The branching Eden brooks ye see
Peeping, and fresh as on the day
When haply Abram's steward went—
Mild Eliezer, musing, say—
By those same banks, to join the tent
In Canaan pitched. From Hermon stray
Cool airs that in a dream of snows
Temper the ardor of the rose;
While yet to moderate and reach
A tone beyond our human speech,
How steals from cloisters of the groves
The ave of the vesper-doves.
Such notes, translated into hues,
Thy wall, Angelico, suffuse,
Whose tender pigments melt from view—
Die down, die out, as sunsets do.
But rustling trees aloft entice
To many a house-top, old and young:
Aerial people! see them throng;
And the moon comes up from Paradise.

But in Jerusalem—not there
Loungers at eve to roof repair
So frequent. Haply two or three
Small quiet groups far off you see,
Or some all uncompanioned one

(Like ship-boy at mast-head alone)
Watching the star-rise. Silently
So Clarel stands, his vaulted room
Opening upon a terrace free,
Lifted above each minor dome
On grade beneath. Glides, glides away
The twilight of the Wailing Day.
The apostate's story fresh in mind,
Fain Clarel here had mused thereon,
But more upon Ruth's lot, so twined

With clinging ill. But every thought
Of Ruth was strangely underrun
By Celio's image. Celio—sought

Vainly in body—now appeared
As in the spiritual part,
Haunting the air, and in the heart.
Back to his charnber Clarel veered,
Seeking that alms which unrest craves
Of slumber alms withheld from him;
For midnight, rending all her graves,
Showed in a vision far and dim
Still Celio and in pallid stress
Fainting amid contending press
Of shadowy fiends and cherubim.
Later, anew he sought the roof;
And started, for not far aloof,
He caught some dubious object dark,
Huddled and hooded, bowed, and set
Under the breast-high parapet,
And glimmering with a dusky spark.
It moved, it murmured. In deep prayer
'Twas Abdon under talith. Rare
That scarf of supplication—old,
Of India stuff, with braid of gold
In cipher. Did the Black Jew keep
The saying—Prayer is more than sleep?
Islam says that. The Hebrew rose,
And, kindled by the starry sky,
In broidered text that mystic flows
The talith gleams. Divested then
He turned, not knowing Clarel nigh,
And would have passed him all unseen.
But Clarel spake. It roused annoy—
An Eastern Jew in rapt employ
Spied by the Gentile. But a word
Dispelled distrust, good-will restored.
"Stay with me," Clarel said; "go not.
A shadow, but I scarce know what—
It haunts me. Is it presage?—Hark!
That piercing cry from out the dark!"
"'Tis for some parted spirit—gone,
Just gone. The custom of the town

That cry is; yea, the watcher's breath
Instant upon the stroke of death."
"Anew! 'Tis like a tongue of flame
Shot from the fissure;" and stood still:

"Can fate the boding thus fulfill?
First ever I, first to disclaim
Such premonitions.—Thrillest yet
I 'Tis over, but we might have met?—
- Hark, hark; again the cry is sped;
For him it is—found now—nay, fled!"

XIX - The Fulfillment

Such passion!—But have hearts forgot
That ties may form where words be not?
The spiritual sympathy
Transcends the social. Which appears
In that presentiment, may be,
Of Clarel's inquietude of fears
Proved just.
Yes, some retreat to win
Even more secluded than the court
The Terra Santa locks within:
Celio had found withdrawn resort
And lodging in the deeper town.

There, by a gasping ill distressed—
Such as attacks the hump-bowed one—
After three days the malady pressed:
He knew it, knew his course was run,
And, turning toward the wall, found rest.
'Twas Syrians watched the parting hour—
And Syrian women shrilled the cry
That wailed it. This, with added store,
Learned Clarel, putting all else by
To get at items of the dead.
Nor, in the throb that casts out fear,
Aught recked he of a scruple here;
But, finding leaves that might bestead,

The jotted journaled thoughts he read.
A second self therein he found,
But stronger—with the heart to brave
All questions on that primal ground
Laid bare by faith's receding wave.
But lo, arrested in event—
Hurried down Hades' steep descent;
Cut off while in progressive stage
Perchance, ere years might more unfold:
Who young dies, leaves life's tale half told.

How then? Is death the book's fly-page?
Is no hereafter? If there be,
Death foots what record? how forestalls
Acquittance in eternity?
Advance too, and through age on age?
Here the tree lies not as it falls;
For howsoe'er in words of man
The word and will of God be feigned,
No incompletion's heaven ordained.
Clarel, through him these reveries ran.

Canto XX - Vale of Ashes

Beyond the city's thin resort
And northward from the Ephraim port
The Vale of Ashes keepeth place.
If stream it have which showeth face,
Thence Kedron issues when in flood:
A pathless dell men seldom trace;
The same which after many a rood
Down deepens by the city wall
Into a glen, where—if we deem
Joel's wild text no Runic dream—
An archangelic trump shall call
The nations of the dead from wreck,
Convene them in one judgment-hall
The hollow of Melchizedek.

That upper glade by quarries old
Reserves for weary ones a seat—
Porches of caves, stone benches cold,
Grateful in sultry clime to meet.
To this secluded spot austere,
Priests bore Talmudic records treat—
The ashes from the altar; here
They laid them, hallowed in release,
Shielded from winds in glade of peace.

From following the bier to end
Hitherward now see Clarel tend;
A dell remote from Celio's mound,
As he for time would shun the ground
So freshly opened for the dead,
Nor linger there while aliens stray
And ceremonious gloom is shed.
Withdrawing to this quiet bay

He felt a natural influence glide
In lenitive through every vein,
And reach the heart, lull heart and brain.
The comrade old was by his side,
And solace shared. But this would pass,
Or dim eclipse would steal thereon,
As over autumn's hill-side grass
The cloud. Howbeit, in freak anon

His Bible he would muttering con,
Then turn, and brighten with a start—
"I hear them, hear them in my heart;
Yea, friend in Christ, I hear them swell—
The trumpets of Immanuel!"
Illusion. But in other hour
When oft he would foretell the flower
And sweets that time should yet bring in,
A happy world, with peace for dower—
This more of interest could win;
For he, the solitary man
Who such a social dream could fan,
What had he known himself of bliss?

And—nearing now his earthly end—
Even that he pledged he needs must miss.
To Clarel now, such musings lend
A vague disturbance, as they wend
Returning thro' the noiseless glade.
But in the gate Nehemiah said,
"My room in court is pleasant, see;
Not yet you've been there come with me."

Canto XXI - By-Places

On Salem's surface undermined,
Lo, present alley, lane or wynd
Obscure, which pilgrims seldom gain
Or tread, who wonted guides retain.
Humble the pilots native there:
Following humbly need ye fare:
Afoot; for never camels pass—
Camels, which elsewhere in the town,
Stalk through the street and brush the gown;
Nor steed, nor mule, nor smaller ass.
Some by-paths, flanked by wall and wall,
Affect like glens. Dismantled, torn,

Disastrous houses, ripe for fall—
Haggard as Horeb, or the rock
Named Hermit, antler of Cape Horn—
Shelter, in chamber grimed, or hall,
The bearded goat-herd's bearded flock;
Or quite abandoned, sold to fear,
Yawn, and like plundered tombs appear.
Here, if alone, strive all ye can,
Needs must ye start at meeting man.
Yet man here harbors, even hc
Harbors like lizard in dry well,
Or stowaway in hull at sea
Down by the keelson; criminal,
Or penitent, or wretch undone,
Or anchorite, or kinless one,

Or wight cast off by kin; or soul
Which anguished from the hunter stole—
Like Emim Bey the Mamaluke.
He—armed, and, happily, mounted well—
Leaped the inhuman citadel
In Cairo; fled—yea, bleeding, broke
Through shouting lanes his breathless way
Into the desert; nor at bay
Even there might stand; but, fox-like, on,
And ran to earth in Zion's town;
Here maimed, disfigured, crouched in den,
And crouching died—securest then.
With these be hearts in each degree
Of craze, whereto some creed is key;
Which, mastered by the awful myth,
Find here, on native soil, the pith;
And leaving a shrewd world behind—
To trances open-eyed resigned—
As visionaries of the Word
Walk like somnambulists abroad.

Canto XXII - Hermitage

Through such retreats of dubious end
Behold the saint and student wend,

Stirring the dust that here may keep
Like that on mummies long asleep
In Theban tomb. Those alleys passed,
A little square they win—a waste

Shut in by towers so hushed, so blind,
So tenantless and left forlorn
As seemed—an ill surmise was born
Of something prowling there behind.
An arch, with key-stone slipped half down
Like a dropped jaw—they enter that;
Repulse nor welcome in the gate:
Climbed, and an upper chamber won.
It looked out through low window small

On other courts of bale shut in,
Whose languishment of crumbling wall
Breathed that despair alleged of sin.
Prediction and fulfillment met
In faint appealings from the rod:
Wherefore forever dost forget—
For so long time forsake, O God?

But Clarel turned him, heedful more
To note the place within. The floor
Rudely was tiled; and little there
A human harbor might express
Save a poor chest, a couch, a chair;
A hermitage how comfortless.
The beams of the low ceiling bare
Were wreck-stuff from the Joppa strand:
Scant the live timber in that land.
Upon the cot the host sat down,
Short breathing, with late travel spent;
And wiping beads from brow and crown,
Essayed a smile, in kindness meant.
But now a little foot was heard
Light coming. On the hush it fell
Like tinkling of the camel-bell
In Uz. "Hark! yea, she comes—my bird!"
Cried Nehemiah who hailed the hap;
"Yea, friend in Christ, quick now ye'll see
God's messenger which feedeth me;"
And rising to the expected tap,
He oped the door. Alone was seen
Ruth with a napkin coarse yet clean,
Folding a loaf. Therewith she bore
A water-pitcher, nothing more.
These alms, the snowy robe and free,
The veil which hid each tress from sight,
Might indicate a vestal white
Or priestess of sweet charity.
The voice was on the lip; but eyes

Arrested in their frank accost,

Checked speech, and looked in opening skies
Upon the stranger. Said the host,
Easing her hands, "Bird, bird, come in:
Well-doing never was a sin—
God bless thee!" In suffusion dim
His eyes filled. She eluding him,
Retreated. "What, and flown?" breathed he:
"Daily this raven comes to me;
But what should make it now so shy?"
The hermit motioned here to share
The loaf with Clarel; who put by
The proffer. So, with Crusoe air
Of castaway on isle in sea
Withdrawn, he broke the unshared bread—
But not before a blessing said:
Loaf in left hand, the right hand raised
Higher, and eyes which heavenward gazed.
Ere long—refection done—the youth
Lured him to talk of things, in range
Linking themselves at last with Ruth.
Her sire he spake of. Here 'twas strange
How o'er the enthusiast stole a change—
A meek superior look in sooth:
"Poor Nathan, did man ever stray
As thou? to Judaize to-day!
To deem the crook of Christ shall yield

To Aaron's staff! to till thy field
In hope that harvest time shall see
Solomon's hook in golden glee
Reaping the ears. Well, well! Me seems—
Heaven help him; dreams, but dreams—dreams, drearr
"But thou, thou too, with faith sincere
Surely believ'st in Jew restored. "
"Yea, as forerunner of our Lord.—
Poor man, he's weak, 'tis even here"
Touching his forehead—"he's amiss."
Clarel scarce found reply to this,
Conjecturing that Nathan too
Must needs hold Nehemiah in view

The same; the which an after-day
Confirmed by proof. But now from sway
Of thoughts he would not have recur,
He slid, and into dream of her
Who late within that cell shed light

Like the angel succorer by night
Of Peter dungeoned. But apace
He turned him, for he heard the breath,
The old man's breath, in sleep. The face
Though tranced, struck not like trance of death
All rigid; not a masque like that,
Iced o'er, which none may penetrate,
Conjecturing of aught below.
Death freezes, but sleep thaws. And so
The inmate lay, some lines revealed—
Effaced, when life from sleep comes back.
And what their import? Be it sealed.
But Clarel felt as in affright
Did Eliphaz the Temanite
When passed the vision ere it spake.
He stole forth, striving with his thought,
Leaving Nehemiah in slumber caught—
Alone, and in an unlocked room,
Safe as a stone in vacant tomb,
Stone none molest, for it is naught.

Canto XXIII - The Close

Next day the wanderer drawing near
Saluting with his humble cheer,
Made Clarel start. Where now the look
That face but late in slumber took?
Had he but dreamed it? It was gone.
But other thoughts were stirring soon,
To such good purpose, that the saint
Through promptings scarce by him divined,
Anew led Clarel thro' constraint
Of inner bye-ways, yet inclined

Away from his peculiar haunt,
And came upon a little close,
One wall whereof a creeper won.
On casement sills, small pots in rows
Showed herb and flower, the shade and sun—
Surprise how blest in town but sere.
OW breathed the guide, "They harbor here
Agar, and my young raven, Ruth.
And, see, there's Nathan, nothing loath,
Just in from Sharon, 'tis his day;
And, yes—the Rabbi in delay."—
The group showed just within the door

Swung open where the creeper led.
In lap the petting mother bore
The half reclining maiden's head—
The stool drawn neighboring the chair;
In front, erect, the father there,
Hollow in cheek, but rugged, brown—
Sharon's red soil upon his shoon—
With zealot gesture urged some plea
Which brought small joy to Agar's eyes,
Whereto turned Ruth's. In scrutiny
Impassive, wrinkled, and how wise
(If wisdom be but craft profound)
Sat the hoar Rabbi. This his guise:
In plaits a head-dress agate-bound,

A sable robe with mystic hem—
Clasps silver, locked in monogram.

An unextinguished lamp they view
Whose flame scarce visibly did sway,
Which having burned till morning dew
Might not be quenched on Saturday
The unaltered sabbath of the Jew.
Struck by the attitudes, the scene,
And loath, a stranger, to advance
Obtrusive, coming so between;
While, in emotion new and strange,
Ruth thrilled him with life's first romance;
Clarel abashed and faltering stood,
With cheek that knew a novel change.
But Nehemiah with air subdued
Made known their presence; and Ruth turned,
And Agar also, and discerned
The stranger, and a settle placed:
Matron and maid with welcome graced
Both visitors, and seemed to find
In travel-talk which here ensued
Relief to burdens of the mind.
But by the sage was Clarel viewed
With stony and unfriendly look—
Fixed inquisition, hard to brook.
And that embarrassment he raised
The Rabbi marked, and colder gazed.
But in redemption from his glance—
For a benign deliverance
On Clarel fell the virgin's eyes,
Pure home of all we seek and prize,
And crossing with their humid ray

The Levite's arid eyes of gray—
But skill is none to word the rest:
To Clarel's heart there came a swell
Like the first tide that ever pressed
Inland, and of a deep did tell.

Thereafter, little speech was had
Save syllables which do but skim;
Even in these, the zealot—made
A slave to one tyrannic whim—
Was scant; while still the sage unkind
Sat a torpedo-fish, with mind
Intent to paralyze, and so
Perchance, make Clarel straight forego
Acquaintance with his flock, at least
With two, whose yearnings—he the priest
More than conjectured—oft did flow
Averse from Salem. None the less
A talismanic gentleness

Maternal welled from Agar faint;
Thro' the sad circle's ill constraint
Her woman's way could yet instill
Her prepossession, her good will;
And when at last they bade good-bye—
The visitors—another eye
Spake at the least of amity.

Canto XXIV - The Gibe

In the south wall, where low it creeps
Crossing the hollow down between
Moriah and Zion, by dust-heaps
Of rubbish in a lonely scene,
A little door there is, and mean—
Such as a stable may befit;
'Tis locked, nor do they open it
Except when days of drought begin,
To let the water-donkeys in
From Rogel. 'Tis in site the gate
Of Scripture named the dung-gate—that
Also (the legends this instill)
Through which from over Kedron's rill—
In fear of rescue should they try
The way less roundabout and shy—

By torch the tip staves Jesus led,
And so thro' back-street hustling sped
To Pilate. Odor bad it has
This gate in story, and alas,
In fact as well, and is in fine
Like ancient Rome's port Esquiline
Wherefrom the scum was cast.—

Next day
Ascending Zion's rear, without
The wall, the saint and Clarel stay
Their feet, being hailed, and by a shout
From one who nigh the small gate stood:
"Ho, ho there, worthy pilgrims, ho!

Acquainted in this neighborhood?
What city's this? town beautiful
Of David? I'm a stranger, know.
'Tis heavy prices here must rule;
Choice house-lot now, what were it worth?
How goes the market?" and more mirth.
Down there into the place unclean
They peer, they see the man therein,
An iron-gray, short, rugged one,
Round shouldered, and of knotty bone;
A hammer swinging in his hand,
And pouch at side, by the ill door.
Him had they chanced upon before
Or rather at a distance seen
Upon the hills, with curious mien
And eyes that—scarce in pious dream
Or sad humility, 'twould seem—
Still earthward bent, would pry and pore.
Perceiving that he shocked the twain,
His head he wagged, and called again,
"What city's this? town beautiful "
No more they heard; but to annul
The cry, here Clarel quick as thought
Turned with the saint and refuge sought
Passing an angle of the wall.
When now at slower pace they went
Clarel observed the sinless one
Turning his Bible-leaves content;
And presently he paused: "Dear son,
The Scripture is fulfilled this day;
Note what these Lamentations say;
The doom the prophet doth rehearse
In chapter second, fifteenth verse:

'All that pass by clap their hands
At thee; they hiss, and wag the head,
Saying, Is this the city'—read,
Thyself here read it where it stands."
Inquisitive he quick obeyed,
Then dull relapsed, and nothing said,

Tho' more he mused, still laboring there
Upward, by arid gullies bare:—
What object sensible to touch
Or quoted fact may faith rely on,
If faith confideth overmuch
That here's a monument in Zion:
Its substance ebbs—see, day and night
The sands subsiding from the height;
In time, absorbed, these grains may help
To form new sea-bed, slug and kelp.
"The gate," cried Nehemiah, "the gate
Of David!" Wending thro' the strait,
And marking that, in common drought,
'Twas yellow waste within as out,
The student mused: The desert, see,
It parts not here, but silently,
Even like a leopard by our side,
It seems to enter in with us—
At home amid men's homes would glide.
But hark! that wail how dolorous:
So grieve the souls in endless dearth;
Yet sounds it human—of the earth!

Canto XXV - Huts

The stone huts face the stony wall
Inside—the city's towering screen—
Leaving a reptile lane between
And streetward not a window small,
Cranny nor loophole least is seen:
Through excess of biting sympathies
So hateful to the people's eyes
Those lepers and their evil nook,
No outlook from it will they brook:
None enter; condolence is none.
That lava glen in Luna's sphere,
More lone than any earthly one—
Whereto they Tycho's name have given—

Not more from visitant is riven
Than this stone lane.
But who crouch here?
Have these been men? these did men greet
As fellows once? It is a scene—
Illusion of time's mirage fleet:
On dry shard-heaps, and things which rot—
Scarce into weeds, for weeds are green—
Backs turned upon their den, they squat,
Some gossips of that tribe unclean.
Time was when Holy Church did take,
Over lands then held by Baldwin's crown,
True care for such for Jesu's sake,
Who (so they read in ages gone)
Even as a leper was foreshown;
And, tho' apart their lot she set,
It was with solemn service yet,
And forms judicial lent their tone:
The sick-mass offered, next was shed
Upon the afflicted human one
The holy water. He was led
Unto the house aloof, his home
Thenceforth. And here, for type of doom,
Some cemetery dust was thrown
Over his head: "Die to the world:
Her wings of hope and fear be furled:
Brother, live now to God alone."
And from the people came the chant:
"My soul is troubled, joy is curbed,
All my bones they are disturbed;
God, thy strength and mercy grant!"
And next, in order due, the priest
Each habit and utensil blessed—
Hair-cloth and barrel, clapper, glove;
And one by one as these were given,
With law's dread charge pronounced in love,
So, link by link, life's chain was riven—
The leper faded in remove.
The dell of isolation here

To match, console, and (could man prove
More than a man) in part endear,
How well had come that smothered text
Which Julian's pagan mind hath vexed—
And ah, for soul that finds it clear:
"He lives forbid;
From him our faces have we hid;
No heart desires him, none redress,

He hath nor form nor comeliness;
For a transgressor he's suspected,
Behold, he is a thing infected,
Smitten of God, by men rejected. "
But otherwise the ordinance flows.
For, moving toward the allotted cell,
Beside the priest the leper goes:
"I've chosen it, here will I dwell."
He's left. At gate the priest puts up
A cross, a can; therein doth drop
The first small alms, which laymen swell.
To aisles returned, the people kneel;
Heart-piercing suppliance—appeal.
But not the austere maternal care
When closed the ritual, ended there
With benediction. Yet to heal,
Rome did not falter, could not faint;
She prompted many a tender saint,

Widow or virgin ministrant.
But chiefly may Sybella here
In chance citation fitly show,
Countess who under Zion's brow
In house of St. John Almoner
Tended the cripples many a year.
Tho' long from Europe's clime be gone
That pest which in the perished age
Could tendance such in love engage,
Still in the East the rot eats on.
Natheless the Syrian leper goes
Unfriended, save that man bestows
(His eye averting) chanceful pence

Then turns, and shares disgust of sense.
Bonds sympathetic bind these three—
Faith, Reverence, and Charity.
If Faith once fail, the faltering mood
Affects—needs must—the sisterhood.

Canto XXVI - The Gate of Zion

As Clarel entered with the guide,
Beset they were by that sad crew—
With inarticulate clamor plied;
And faces, yet defacements too,
Appealed to them; but could not give

Expression. There, still sensitive,
Our human nature, deep inurned
In voiceless visagelessness, yearned.
Behold, proud worm (if such can be),
What yet may come, yea, even to thee.
Who knoweth? canst forecast the fate
In infinite ages? Probe thy state:
Sinless art thou? Then these sinned not.
These, these are men; and thou art—what?
For Clarel, turning in affright,
Fain would his eyes renounce the light.
But Nehemiah held on his path
Mild and unmoved—scarce seemed to heed
The suitors, or deplore the scath—
His soul pre-occupied and freed
From actual objects thro' the sway
Of visionary scenes intense—
The wonders of a mystic day
And Zion's old magnificence.
Nor hither had he come to show
The leper-huts, but only so
To visit once again the hill
And gate Davidic.
In ascent
They win the port's high battlement,

And thence in sweep they view at will
That theatre of heights which hold
As in a Coliseum's fold
They guarded Zion. They command
The Mount of Solomon's Offense,
The Crag of Evil Council, and
Iscariot's gallows-eminence.
Pit too they mark where long ago
Dull fires of refuse, shot below,
The city's litter, smouldering burned,
Clouding the glen with smoke impure,
And griming the foul shapes obscure
Of dismal chain-gangs in their shame
Raking the garbage thither spurned:
Tophet the place—transferred, in name,
To penal Hell.
But shows there naught
To win here a redeeming thought?
Yes: welcome in its nearer seat
The white Caenaculum they greet,
Where still an upper room is shown—
In dream avouched the very one

Wherein the Supper first was made
And Christ those words of parting said,
Those words of love by loved St. John
So tenderly recorded. Ah,

They be above us like a star,
Those Paschal words.
But they descend;
And as within the wall they wend,
A Horror hobbling on low crutch
Draws near, but still refrains from touch.
Before the saint in low estate
He fawns, who with considerate
Mild glance regards him. Clarel shrank:
And he, is he of human rank?—
"Knowest thou him?" he asked.—"Yea, yea,
And beamed on that disfeatured clay:
"Toulib, to me? to Him are due

These thanks—the God of me and you
And all; to whom His own shall go
In Paradise and be re-clad,
Transfigured like the morning glad.—
Yea, friend in Christ, this man I know,
This fellow-man."—And afterward
The student from true sources heard
How Nehemiah had proved his friend,
Sole friend even of that trunk of woe,
When sisters failed him in the end.

Canto XXVII - Matron and Maid

Days fleet. No vain enticements lure
Clarel to Agar's roof. Her tact
Prevailed: the Rabbi might not act
His will austere. And more and more
A prey to one devouring whim,
Nathan yet more absented him.
Welcome the matron ever had
For Clarel. Was the youth not one
New from the clime she doated on?
And if indeed an exile sad
By daisy in a letter laid
Reminded be of home-delight,
Tho' there first greeted by the sight
Of that transmitted flower—how then

Not feel a kin emotion bred
At glimpse of face of countryman
Tho' stranger? Yes, a Jewess—born
In Gentile land where nature's wreath
Exhales the first creation's breath—
The waste of Judah made her lorn.
The student, sharing not her blood,
Nearer in tie of spirit stood
Than he she called Rabboni. So
In Agar's liking did he grow—
Deeper in heart of Ruth; and learned

The more how both for freedom yearned;
And much surmised, too, left unsaid
By the tried mother and the maid.
Howe'er dull natures read the signs
Where untold grief a hermit pines—
The anxious, strained, weak, nervous air
Of trouble, which like shame may wear
Her gaberdine; though soul in feint
May look pathetic self-restraint,
For ends pernicious; real care,
Sorrow made dumb where duties move,
Never eluded love, true love,
A deep diviner.
Here, for space
The past of wife and daughter trace.
Of Agar's kin for many an age
Not one had seen the heritage
Of Judah; Gentile lands detained.
So, while they clung to Moses' lore
Far from the land his guidance gained,
'Twas Eld's romance, a treasured store
Like plate inherited. In fine
It graced, in seemly way benign,
That family feeling of the Jew,
Which hallowed by each priestly rite,
Makes home a temple—sheds delight

Naomi ere her trial knew.
Happy was Agar ere the seas
She crossed for Zion. Pride she took—
Pride, if in small felicities—
Pride in her little court, a nook
Where morning-glories starred the door:
So sweet without, so snug within.
At sunny matin meal serene
Her damask cloth she'd note. It bore

In Hebrew text about the hem,
Mid broidered cipher and device
IF I FORGET THEE, O JERUSALEM!
And swam before her humid eyes,

In rainbowed distance, Paradise.
Faith, ravished, followed Fancy's path
In more of bliss than nature hath.
But ah, the dream to test by deed,
To seek to handle the ideal
And make a sentiment serve need:
To try to realize the unreal!
'Twas not that Agar reasoned—nay,
She did but feel, true woman's way.
What solace from the desert win
Far from known friends, familiar kin?
How nearer God? The chanted Zion
Showed graves, but graves to gasp and die on.
Nathan, her convert, for his sake
Grief had she stifled long; but now,
The nursling one lay pale and low.
Oft of that waxen face she'd think
Beneath the stones; her heart would sink
And in hard bitterness repine,
"Slim grass, poor babe, to grave of thine!"

Ruth, too, when here a child she came,
Would blurt in reckless childhood's way,
"'Tis a bad place." But the sad dame
Would check; and, as the maiden grew,
Counsel she kept—too much she knew.
But how to give her feelings play?
With cherished pots of herbs and flowers
She strove to appease the hungry hours;
Each leaf bedewed with many a tear
For Gentile land, how green and dear!
What tho' the dame and daughter both
In synagogue, behind the grate
Dividing sexes, oftimes sat?
It was with hearts but chill and loath;
Never was heaven served by that
Cold form.—With Clarel seemed to come
A waftage from the fields of home,

Crossing the wind from Judah's sand,
Reviving Agar, and of power
To make the bud in Ruth expand
With promise of unfolding hour.

Canto XXVIII - Tomb and Fountain

Clarel and Ruth—might it but be
That range they could green uplands free
By gala orchards, when they fling
Their bridal favors, buds of Spring;
And, dreamy in her morning swoon,
The lady of the night, the moon,
Looks pearly as the blossoming;
And youth and nature's fond accord
Wins Eden back, that tales abstruse
Of Christ, the crucified, Pain's Lord,
Seem foreign—forged—incongruous.

Restrictions of that Eastern code
Immured the maiden. From abode
Frequent nor distant she withdrew
Except with Jewess, scarce with Jew.
So none the less in former mode,
Nehemiah still with Clarel went,
Who grew in liking and content

In company of one whose word
Babbled of Ruth "My bird—God's bird."

The twain were one mild morning led
Out to a waste where beauty clings,
Vining a grot how doubly dead:
The rifled Sepulcher of Kings.
Hewn from the rock a sunken space
Conducts to garlands—fit for vasc
In sculptured frieze above a tomb:
Palm leaves, pine apples, grapes. These bloom,

Involved in death—to puzzle us—
As 'twere thy line, Theocritus,
Dark Joel's text of terror threading:
Yes, strange that Pocahontas-wedding
Of contraries in old belief—
Hellenic cheer, Hebraic grief.
The homicide Herods, men aver,
Inurned behind that wreathage were.

But who is he uncovered seen,
Profound in shadow of the tomb

Reclined, with meditative mien
Intent upon the tracery?
A low wind waves his Lydian hair:
A funeral man, yet richly fair—
Fair as the sabled violets be.
The frieze and this secluded one,
Retaining each a separate tone,
Beauty yet harmonized in grace
And contrast to the barren place.
But noting that he was discerned,
Salute the stranger made, then turned
And shy passed forth in obvious state
Of one who would keep separate.

Those cells explored, thro' dale they paced
Downward, and won Moriah's walls
And seated them. Clarel recalls
The colonnades that Herod traced—
Herod, magnific Idumaean—
In marble along the mountain flank:
Column on column, rank on rank
Above the valley Tyropeeon.
Eastward, in altitude they view
Across Jehoshaphat, a crag
Of sepulchers and huts. Thereto
They journey. But awhile they lag
Beneath, to mark the tombs in row
Pierced square along the gloomy steep
In beetling broadside, and with show

' Of port-holes in black battle-ship.
They climb; and Clarel turning saw
yheir late resort, the hill of law—
Moriah, above the Kedron's bed;
And, turreting his aged head,
The angle of King David's wall—
Acute seen here, here too best scanned,
As 'twere that cliff, tho' not so tall,
Nor tempest-sculptured therewithal,
Envisaged in Franconian land,
Fyhe marvel of the Pass.
Anon
A call he hears behind, in note
Familiar, being man's; remote
No less, and strange in hollowed tone
As 'twere a voice from out the tomb.
A tomb it is; and he in gloom
Of porch there biddeth them begone.

Clings to his knee a toddling one
Bewildered poising in wee hand
A pictured page—Nehemiah's boon—
He passive in the sun at stand.
Morosely then the Arab turns,
Snatches the gift, and drops and spurns.
As down now from the crag they wend

Reverted glance see Clarel lend:
Thou guest of Death, which in his house
Sleep'st nightly, mayst thou not espouse
His daughter, Peace?
Aslant they come
Where, hid in shadow of the rocks,
Stone steps descend unto Siloam.
Proof to the fervid noon-day tide
Reflected from the glen's steep side
Moist ledge with ledge here interlocks,
Vaulting a sunken grotto deep.
Down there, as quiet as in sleep,
Anew the stranger they descried
Sitting upon a step full low,
Watching the fountain's troubled tide
Which after ebb began to flow,
Gurgling from viewless caves. The lull
Broke by the flood is wonderful.
Science explains it. Bides no less
The true, innate mysteriousness.
Through him there might the vision flit
Of angel in Bethesda's pool
With porches five, so troubling it
That whoso bathed then was made whole?
Or, by an equal dream beguiled,
Did he but list the fountain moan
Like Ammon's in the Libyan wild,
For muse and oracle both gone?
By chance a jostled pebble there
Slipped from the surface down the stair.
It jarred—it broke the brittle spell:
Siloam was but a rural well.

Clarel who could again but shun
To obtrude on the secluded one,
Turned to depart.—"Ere yet we go,"
Said Nehemiah, "I will below:
Dim be mine eyes, more dim they grow:
I'll wash them in these waters cool,
As did the blind the Master sent,

And who came seeing from this pool;"
And down the grotto-stairs he went.
The stranger, just ascending, stood;
And, as the votary laved his eyes,
He marked, looked up, and Clarel viewed,
And they exchanged quick sympathies
Though but in glance, moved by that act
Of one whose faith transfigured fact.
A bond seemed made between them there;
And presently the trio fare
Over Kedron, and in one accord
Of quietude and chastened tone
Approach the spot, tradition's own,
For ages held the garden of Our Lord.

Canto XXIX - The Recluse

Ere yet they win that verge and line,
Reveal the stranger. Name him—Vine.
His home to tell—kin, tribe, estate—
Would naught avail. Alighting grow,
As on the tree the mistletoe,
All gifts unique. In seeds of fate
Borne on the winds these emigrate
And graft the stock.
Vine's manner shy
A clog, a hindrance might imply;
A lack of parlor-wont. But grace
Which is in substance deep and grain
May, peradventure, well pass by
The polish of veneer. No trace
Of passion's soil or lucre's stain,
Though life was now half ferried o'er.
If use he served not, but forbore—
Such indolence might still but pine
In dearth of rich incentive high:
Apollo slave in Mammon's mine?
Better Admetus' shepherd lie.
A charm of subtle virtue shed
A personal influence coveted,
Whose source was difficult to tell

As ever was that perfumed spell
Of Paradise-flowers invisible
Which angels round Cecilia bred.
A saint then do we here unfold?

Nay, the ripe flush, Venetian mould
Evinced no nature saintly fine,
But blood like swart Vesuvian wine.
What cooled the current? Under cheer
Of opulent softness, reigned austere
Control of self. Flesh, but scarce pride,
Was curbed: desire was mortified;
But less indeed by moral sway
Than doubt if happiness thro' clay

Be reachable. No sackclothed man;
Howbeit, in sort Carthusian
Tho' born a Sybarite. And yet
Not beauty might he all forget,
The beauty of the world, and charm:
He prized it tho' it scarce might warm.
Like to the nunnery's denizen
His virgin soul communed with men
But thro' the wicket. Was it clear
This coyness bordered not on fear—
Fear or an apprehensive sense?
Not wholly seemed it diffidence
Recluse. Nor less did strangely wind
Ambiguous elfishness behind
All that: an Ariel unknown.
It seemed his very speech in tone
Betrayed disuse. Thronged streets astir
To Vine but ampler cloisters were.
Cloisters? No monk he was, allow;
But gleamed the richer for the shade
About him, as in sombre glade
Of Virgil's wood the Sibyl's Golden Bough.

Canto XXX - The Site of the Passion

And wherefore by the convents be
Gardens? Ascetics roses twine?
Nay, but there is a memory.
Within a garden walking see
The angered God. And where the vine
And olive in the darkling hours
Inweave green sepulchers of bowers—
Who, to defend us from despair,
Pale undergoes the passion there
In solitude? Yes, memory
Links Eden and Gethsemane;

So that not meaningless in sway
Gardens adjoin the convents gray.

On Salem's hill in Solomon's years
Of gala, O the happy town!
In groups the people sauntered down,
And, Kedron crossing, lightly wound
Where now the tragic grove appears,
Then palmy, and a pleasure-ground.

The student and companions win
The wicket—pause, and enter in.
By roots strapped down in fold on fold—
Gnarled into wens and knobs and knees—
In olives, monumental trees,
The Pang's survivors they behold.
A wizened blue fruit drops from them,
Nipped harvest of Jerusalem.
Wistful here Clarel turned toward Vine,
And would have spoken; but as well
Hail Dathan swallowed in the minc-
Tradition, legend, lent such spell
And rapt him in remoteness so.
Meanwhile, in shade the olives throw,
Nehemiah pensive sat him down
And turned the chapter in St John.
What frame of mind may Clarel woo?

He the night-scene in picture drew—
The band which came for sinless blood
With swords and staves, a multitude.
They brush the twigs, small birds take wing,
The dead boughs crackle, lanterns swing
Till lo, they spy them thro' the wood.
"Master!"—'Tis Judas. Then the kiss.
And He, He falters not at this—
Speechless, unspeakably submiss:
The fulsome serpent on the cheek
Sliming: endurance more than meek—

Endurance of the fraud foreknown,
And fiend-heart in the human one.
Ah, now the pard on Clarel springs:
The Passion's narrative plants stings.
To break away, he turns and views
The white-haired under olive bowed
Immersed in Scripture; and he woos—

"Whate'er the chapter, read aloud."
The saint looked up, but with a stare
Absent and wildered, vacant there.
As part to kill time, part for task
Some shepherd old pores over book—
Shelved farm-book of his life forepast
When he bestirred him and amassed;
If chance one interrupt, and ask—
What read you? he will turn a look
Which shows he knows not what he reads,
Or knowing, he but weary heeds,
Or scarce remembers; here much so
With Nehemiah, dazed out and low.
And presently—to intercept—
Over Clarel, too, strange numbness crept.
A monk, custodian of the ground,
Drew nigh, and showed him by the steep
The rock or legendary mound
Where James and Peter fell asleep.
Dully the pilgrim scanned the spot,
Nor spake.—"Signor, and think'st thou not
'Twas sorrow brought their slumber on?
St. Luke avers no sluggard rest:
Nay, but excess of feeling pressed
Till ache to apathy was won."
To Clarel 'twas no hollow word.
Experience did proof afford.
For Vine, aloof he loitered—shrunk
In privity and shunned the monk.
Clarel awaited him. He came
The shadow of his previous air
Merged in a settled neutral frame

Assumed, may be. Would Vine disclaim
All sympathy the youth might share?

About to leave, they turn to look
For him but late estranged in book:
Asleep he lay; the face bent down
Viewless between the crossing arms,
One slack hand on the good book thrown
In peace that every care becharms.
Then died the shadow off from Vine:
A spirit seemed he not unblest
As here he made a quiet sign
Unto the monk: Spare to molest;
Let this poor dreamer take his rest,
His fill of rest.

But now at stand
Who there alertly glances up
By grotto of the Bitter Cup—
Spruce, and with volume light in hand
Bound smartly, late in reference scanned?
Inquisitive Philistine: lo,
Tourists replace the pilgrims so.
At peep of that brisk dapper man
Over Vine's face a ripple ran
Of freakish mockery, elfin light;
Whereby what thing may Clarel see?

O angels, rescue from the sight!
Paul Pry? and in Gethsemane?
He shrunk the thought of it to fan;
Nor liked the freak in Vine that threw
Such a suggestion into view;
Nor less it hit that fearful man.

Canto XXXI - Rolfe

The hill above the garden here
They rove; and chance ere long to meet
A second stranger, keeping cheer

Apart. Trapper or pioneer
He looked, astray in Judah's seat—
Or one who might his business ply
On waters under tropic sky.
Perceiving them as they drew near,
He rose, removed his hat to greet,
Disclosing so in shapely sphere
A marble brow over face embrowned:
So Sunium by her fane is crowned.
One read his superscription clear—
A genial heart, a brain austere
And further, deemed that such a man
Though given to study, as might seem,
Was no scholastic partisan
Or euphonist of Academe,
But supplemented Plato's theme
With daedal life in boats and tents,
A messmate of the elements;
And yet, more bronzed in face than mind,
Sensitive still and frankly kind—
Too frank, too unreserved, may be,

And indiscreet in honesty.
But what implies the tinge of soil—
Like tarnish on Pizarro's spoil,
Precious in substance rudely wrought,
Peruvian plate—which here is caught?
What means this touch of the untoward
In aspect hinting nothing froward?

From Baalbec, for a new sojourn,
To Jewry Rolfe had made return;
To Jewry's inexhausted shore
Of barrenness, where evermore
Some lurking thing he hoped to gdill—
Slip quite behind the parrot-lore
Conventional, and what attain?
Struck by each clear or latent sign
Expressive in the stranger's air,
The student glanced from him to Vine:

Peers, peers—yes, needs that these must pair.
Clarel was young. In promise fine,
To him here first were brought together
Exceptional natures, of a weather
Strange as the tropics with strange trees,
Strange birds, strange fishes, skies and seas,
To one who in some meager land
His bread wins by the horny hand.
What now may hap? what outcome new
Elicited by contact true—
Frank, cordial contact of the twain?
Crude wonderment, and proved but vain.
If average mortals social be,
And yet but seldom truly meet,
Closing like halves of apple sweet—
How with the rarer in degree?
The informal salutation done,
Vine into his dumb castle went—
Not as all parley he would shun,
But looking down from battlement,
Ready, if need were, to accord
Reception to the other's word,—
Nay, far from wishing to decline,
And neutral not without design,
May be.—
"Look, by Christ's belfry set,

Appears the Moslem minaret!"
So—to fill trying pause alone—

Cried Rolfe; and o'er the deep defile
Of Kedron, pointed toward the Town
Where, thronged about by many a pile
Monastic, but no vernal bower,
The Saracen shaft and Norman tower
In truce stand guard beside that Dome
Which canopies the Holy's home:
"The tower looks lopped; it shows forlorn—
A stunted oak whose crown is shorn
But see, palm-like the minaret stands
Superior, and the tower commands."

"Yon shaft," said Clarel, "seems ill-placed."
"Ay, seems; but 'tis for memory based.
The story's known: how Omar there
After the town's surrender meek—
Hallowed to him, as dear to Greek—
Clad in his clouts of camel's hair,
And with the Patriarch robed and fine
Walking beneath the dome divine,
When came the Islam hour for prayer
Declined to use the carpet good
Spread for him in the church, but stood
Without, even yonder where is set
The monumental minaret;
And, earnest in true suppliance cried,
Smiting his chest: 'Me overrule!
Allah, to me be merciful!'
'Twas little shared he victor-pride
Though victor. So the church he saved
Of purpose from that law engraved
Which prompt transferred to Allah sole
Each fane where once his rite might roll.
Long afterward, the town being stormed
By Christian knights, how ill conformed
The butchery then to Omar's prayer
And heart magnanimous. But spare."

Response they looked; and thence he warmed:
"Yon gray Cathedral of the Tomb,
Who reared it first? a woman weak,
A second Mary, first to seek
In pagan darkness which had come,
The place where they had laid the Lord:
Queen Helena, she traced the site,
And cleared the ground, and made it bright
With all that zeal could then afford.
But Constantine—there falls the blight!

The mother's warm emotional heart,
Subserved it still the son's cold part?
Even he who, timing well the tide,

Laced not the Cross upon Rome's flag
Supreme, till Jove began to lag
Behind the new religion's stride.
And Helena—ah, may it be
The saint herself not quite was free
From that which in the years bygone,
Made certain stately dames of France,
Such as the fair De Maintenon,
To string their rosaries of pearl,
And found brave chapels—sweet romance:
Coquetry of the borrowed curl?—
You let me prate."
                "Nay, nay—go on,"
Cried Clarel, yet in such a tone
It showed disturbance.—
                        "Laud the dame:
Her church, admit, no doom it fears.
Unquelled by force of battering years—
Years, years and sieges, sword and flame;
Fallen—rebuilt, to fall anew;
By armies shaken, earthquake too;
Lo, it abides—if not the same,
In self-same spot. Last time 'twas burnt
The Rationalist a lesson learnt.
But you know all."—
                    "Nay, not the end,"

Said Vine. And Clarel, "We attend."
"Well, on the morrow never shrunk
From wonted rite the steadfast monk,
Though hurt and even maimed were some
By crash of the ignited dome.
Staunch stood the walls. As friars profess
(And not in fraud) the central cell—
Christ's tomb and faith's last citadel—
The flames did tenderly caress,
Nor harm; while smoking, smouldering beams,
Fallen across, lent livid gleams
To Golgotha. But none the less
In robed procession of his God

The mitred one the cinders trod;
Before the calcined altar there
The host he raised; and hymn and prayer

Went up from ashes. These, ere chill,
Away were brushed; and trowel shrill
And hod and hammer came in place.
'Tis now some three score years ago.
"In Lima's first convulsion so,
When shock on shock had left slim trace
Of hundred temples; and—in mood
Of malice dwelling on the face
Itself has tortured and subdued
To uncomplaint—the cloud pitch-black
Lowered o'er the rubbish; and the land
Not less than sea, did countermand
Her buried corses—heave them back;
And flocks and men fled on the track
Which wins the Andes; then went forth
The prelate with intrepid train
Rolling the anthem 'mid the rain
Of ashes white. In rocking plain
New boundaries staked they, south and north,
For ampler piles. These stand. In cheer
The priest reclaimed the quaking sphere.
Hold it he shall, so long as spins
This star of tragedies, this orb of sins."
"That," Clarel said, "is not my mind.
Rome's priest forever rule the world?"
"The priest, I said. Though some be hurled
From anchor, nor a haven find;
Not less religion's ancient port,
Till the crack of doom, shall be resort
In stress of weather for mankind.
Yea, long as children feel affright
In darkness, men shall fear a God;
And long as daisies yield delight
Shall see His footprints in the sod.
Is't ignorance? This ignorant state
Science doth but elucidate—

Deepen, enlarge. But though 'twere made
Demonstrable that God is not—
What then? it would not change this lot:
The ghost would haunt, nor could be laid."
Intense he spake, his eyes of blue
Altering, and to eerie hue,
Like Tyrrhene seas when overcast;
The which Vine noted, nor in joy,
Inferring thence an ocean-waste
Of earnestness without a buoy:
An inference which afterward

Acquaintance led him to discard
Or modify, or not employ.
Clarel ill-relished.
Rolfe, in tone
Half elegiac, thus went on:
"Phyla, upon thy sacred ground
Osiris' broken tomb is found:
A god how good, whose good proved vain—
In strife with bullying Python slain.
For long the ritual chant or moan
Of pilgrims by that mystic stone
Went up, even much as now ascend
The liturgies of yearning prayer
To one who met a kindred end—
Christ, tombed in turn, and worshiped there,"

And pointed.—"Hint you," here asked Vine,
"In Christ Osiris met decline
Anew?"—"Nay, nay; and yet, past doubt,
Strange is that text St. Matthew won
From gray Hosea in sentence: Out
Of Egypt have I called my son. "
Here Clarel spake, and with a stir
Not all assured in eager plight:
"But does not Matthew there refer
Only to the return from flight,
Flight into Egypt?"—"May be so,"
Said Rolfe; "but then Hosea?—Nay,
We'll let it pass."—And fell delay

Of talk; they mused.—
"To Cicero,"
Rolfe sudden said, "is a long way
From Matthew; yet somehow he comes
To mind here—he and his fine tomes,
Which (change the gods) would serve to read
For modern essays. And indeed
His age was much like ours: doubt ran,
Faith flagged; negations which sufficed
Lawyer, priest, statesman, gentleman,
Not yet being popularly prized,
The augurs hence retained some state—
Which served for the illiterate.
Still, the decline so swiftly ran
From stage to stage, that To Believe,
Except for slave or artisan,
Seemed heresy. Even doubts which met
Horror at first, grew obsolete,

And in a decade. To bereave
Of founded trust in Sire Supreme,
Was a vocation. Sophists throve—
Each weaving his thin thread of dream
Into the shroud for Numa's Jove.
Caesar his atheism avowed
Before the Senate. But why crowd
Examples here: the gods were gone.
Tully scarce dreamed they could be won
Back into credence; less that earth
Ever could know yet mightier birth
Of deity. He died. Christ came.
And, in due hour, that impious Rome,
Emerging from vast wreck and shame,
Held the fore front of Christendom.
The inference? the lesson?—come:
Let fools count on faith's closing knell—
Time, God, are inexhaustible.—
But what? so earnest? ay, again."
"Hard for a fountain to refrain,"
Breathed Vine. Was that but irony?

At least no envy in the strain.
Rolfe scarce remarked, or let go by.
For Clarel—when ye, meeting, scan
In waste the Bagdad caravan,
And solitude puts on the stir,
Clamor, dust, din of Nineveh,
As horsemen, camels, footmen all,
Soldier and merchant, free and thrall,
Pour by in tide processional;
So to the novice streamed along
Rolfe's filing thoughts, a wildering throng.
Their sway he owned. And yet how Vine—
Who breathed few words, or gave dumb sign—
Him more allured, suggestive more
Of choicer treasure, rarer store
Reserved, like Kidd's doubloons long sought
Without the wand.
The ball of thought
And chain yet dragging, on they strained
Oblique along the upland—slow
And mute, until a point they gained
Where devotees will pause, and know
A tenderness, may be. Here then,
While tarry now these pilgrim men,
The interval let be assigned
A niche for image of a novel mind.

Canto XXXII - Of Rama

That Rama whom the Indian sung—
A god he was, but knew it not;
Hence vainly puzzled at the wrong
Misplacing him in human lot.
Curtailment of his right he bare
Rather than wrangle; but no less
Was taunted for his tameness there.
A fugitive without redress,
He never the Holy Spirit grieved,

Nor the divine in him bereaved,
Though what that was he might not guess.

Live they who, like to Rama, led
Unspotted from the world aside,
Like Rama are discredited—
Like him, in outlawry abide?
May life and fable so agree?—
The innocent if lawless elf,
Etherial in virginity,
Retains the consciousness of self.
Though black frost nip, though white frost chill,
Nor white frost nor the black may kill
The patient root, the vernal sense
Surviving hard experience
As grass the winter. Even that curse
Which is the wormwood mixed with gall—
Better dependent on the worse—
Divine upon the animal—
That can not make such natures fall.
Though yielding easy rein, indeed,
To impulse which the fibers breed,
Nor quarreling with indolence;
Shall these the cup of grief dispense
Deliberate to any heart?
Not craft they know, nor envy's smart.
Theirs be the thoughts that dive and skim,
Theirs the spiced tears that overbrim,
And theirs the dimple and the lightsome whim.
Such natures, and but such, have got
Familiar with strange things that dwell
Repressed in mortals; and they tell
Of riddles in the prosiest lot.

Mince ye some matter for faith's sake
And heaven's good name? 'Tis these shall make
Revolt there, and the gloss disclaim.
They con the page kept down with those
Which Adam's secret frame disclose,
And Eve's; nor dare dissent from truth
Although disreputable, sooth.

The riches in them be a store
Unmerchantable in the ore.
No matter: "'Tis an open mine:
Dig; find ye gold, why, make it thine.
The shrewder knack hast thou, the gift:
Smelt then, and mold, and good go with thy thrift."

Was ever earth-born wight like this?
Ay—in the verse, may be, he is.

Canto XXXIII - By the Stone

Over against the Temple here
A monastery unrestored—
Named from Prediction of Our Lord—
Crumbled long since. Outlying near,
Some stones remain, which seats afford:
And one, the fond traditions state,
Is that whereon the Saviour sate
And prophesied, and sad became
To think, what, under sword and flame,
The proud Jerusalem should be,
Then spread before him sunnily—
Pillars and palms—the white, the green—
Marble enfoliaged, a fair scene;
But now—a vision here conferred
Pale as Pompeii disinterred.

Long Rolfe, on knees his elbows resting
And head enlocked in hands upright,
Sat facing it in steadfast plight
And brooded on that town slow wasting.
"And here," he said, "here did He sit—
In leafy covert, say—Beheld
The city, and wept over it:
Luke's words, and hard to be excelled,
So just the brief expression there:
Truth's rendering. "—With earnest air,

More he threw out, in kind the same,
The which did Clarel ponder still;
For though the words might frankness claim,
With reverence for site and name;
No further went they, nor could fill
Faith's measure—scarce her dwindled gill
Now standard. On the plain of Troy
(Mused Clarel) as one might look down
From Gargarus with quiet joy
In verifying Homer's sites,
Yet scarce believe in Venus' crown
And rescues in those Trojan fights
Whereby she saved her supple son;
So Rolfe regards from these wan heights
Yon walls and slopes to Christians dear.
Much it annoyed him and perplexed:
Than free concession so sincere—
Concession due both site and text—
Dissent itself would less appear
To imply negation.
But anon
They mark in groups, hard by the gate
Which overlooks Jehoshaphat,
Some Hebrew people of the town.
"Who marvels that outside they come
Since few within have seemly home,"
Said Rolfe; "they chat there on the seats,
But seldom gossip in their streets.
Who here may see a busy one?
Where's naught to do not much is done.
How live they then? what bread can be?
In almost every country known
Rich Israelites these kinsmen own:
The hat goes round the world. But see!"
Moved by his words, their eyes more reach
Toward that dull group. Dwarfed in the dream
Of distance sad, penguins they seem
Drawn up on Patagonian beach.

"O city," Rolfe cried; "house on moor,
With shutters burst and blackened door—
Like that thou showest; and the gales
Still round thee blow the Banshee-wails:
Well might the priest in temple start,
Hearing the voice—'Woe, we depart!' "

Clarel gave ear, albeit his glance
Diffident skimmed Vine's countenance,

As mainly here he interest took
In all the fervid speaker said,
Reflected in the mute one's look:
A face indeed quite overlaid
With tremulous meanings, which evade
Or shun regard, nay, hardly brook
Fraternal scanning.
Rolfe went on:
"The very natives of the town
Methinks would turn from it and flee
But for that curse which is its crown—
That curse which clogs so, poverty.
See them, but see yon cowering men:
The brood—the brood without the hen!"—

"City, that dost the prophets stone,
How oft against the judgment dread,
How often would I fain have spread
My wings to cover thee, mine own;
And ye would not! Had'st thou but known
The things which to thy peace belong!"
Nehemiah it was, rejoining them—
Gray as the old Jerusalem
Over which how earnestly he hung.
But him the seated audience scan
As he were sole surviving man
Of tribe extinct or world. The ray
Which lit his features, died away;
He flagged; and, as some trouble moved,
Apart and aimlessly he roved.

Canto XXXIV - They Tarry

"How solitary on the hill
Sitteth the city; and how still—
How still!" From Vine the murmur came—
A cadence, as it were compelled
Even by the picture's silent claim.
That said, again his peace he held,
Biding, as in a misty rain
Some motionless lone fisherman
By mountain brook. But Rolfe: "Thy word
Is Jeremiah's, and here well heard.
Ay, seer of Anathoth, behold,
Yon object tallies with thy text.
How then? Stays reason quite unvexed?

Fulfillment here but falleth cold.
That stable proof which man would fold,
How may it be derived from things
Subject to change and vanishings?
But let that pass. All now's revised:
Zion, like Rome, is Niebuhrized.
Yes, doubt attends. Doubt's heavy hand
Is set against us; and his brand
Still warreth for his natural lord—
King Common-Place—whose rule abhorred
Yearly extends in vulgar sway,
Absorbs Atlantis and Cathay;
Ay, reaches toward Diana's moon,
Affirming it a clinkered blot,
Deriding pale Endymion.
Since thus he aims to level all,
The Milky Way he'll yet allot
For Appian to his Capital.
Then tell, tell then, what charm may save
Thy marvel, Palestine, from grave
Whereto winds many a bier and pall
Of old Illusion? What for earth?
Ah, change irreverent,—at odds
With goodly customs, gracious gods;
New things elate so thrust their birth
Up through dejection of the old,
As through dead sheaths; is here foretold
The consummation of the past,
And gairish dawning of a day
Whose noon not saints desire to stay—
And hardly I? Who brake love's fast
With Christ—with what strange lords may sup?
The reserves of time seem marching up.
But, nay: what novel thing may be,
No germ being new? By Fate's decree
Have not earth's vitals heaved in change
Repeated? some wild element
Or action been evolved? the range
Of surface split? the deeps unpent?
Continents in God's caldrons cast?
And this without effecting so
The neutralizing of the past,
Whose rudiments persistent flow,
From age to age transmitting, own,
The evil with the good—the taint
Deplored in Solomon's complaint.
Fate's pot of ointment! Wilt have done,
Lord of the fly, god of the grub?

Need'st foul all sweets, thou Beelzebub?"

He ended.—To evade or lay
Deductions hard for tender clay,
Clarel recalled each prior word
Of Rolfe which scarcely kept accord,
As seemed, with much dropped latterly.
or Vine, he twitched from ground a weed,
Apart then picked it, seed by seed.
Ere long they rise, and climbing greet
thing preeminent in seat,
Whose legend still can touch the heart:
prompted one there to impart
chapter of the Middle Age—
Which next to give. But let the page

The narrator's rambling way forget,
And make to run in even flow
His interrupted tale. And let
Description brief the site foreshow.

Canto XXXV - Arculf and Adamnan

In spot revered by myriad men,
Whence, as alleged, Immanuel rose
Into the heaven—receptive then—
A little plastered tower is set,
Pale in the light that Syria knows,
Upon the peak of Olivet.
'Tis modern—a replacement, note,
For ample pile of years remote,
Nor yet ill suits in dwindled bound,
Man's faith retrenched. 'Twas Hakeem's deed,
Mad Caliph (founder still of creed
Long held by tribes not unrenowned)
Who erst the pastoral hight discrowned
Of Helena's church. Woe for the dome,
And many a goodly temple more,
Which hither lured from Christendom
The child-like pilgrim throngs of yore.
'Twas of that church, so brave erewhile—
Blest land-mark on the Olive Hight—
Which Arculf told of in the isle
Iona. Shipwrecked there in sight,
The palmer dragged they from the foam,
The Culdees of the abbey fair—

Him shelter yielding and a home.
In guerdon for which love and care
Received in Saint Columba's pile,
With travel-talk he did beguile
Their eve of Yule.
The tempest beat;
It shook the abbey's founded seat,
Rattling the crucifix on wall;

And thrice was heard the clattering fall
Of gable-tiles. But host and guest,
Abbot and palmer, took their rest
Inside monastic ingle tall.
What unto them were those lashed seas?
Or Patmos or the Hebrides,
The isles were God's.
It was the time
The church in Jewry dwelt at ease
Tho' under Arabs—Omar's prime—
Penultimate of pristine zeal,
While yet throughout faith's commonweal
The tidings had not died away—
Not yet had died into dismay
Of dead, dead echoes that recede:
Glad tidings of great joy indeed,
Thrilled to the shepherds on the sward—
"Behold, to you is born this day
A Saviour, which is Christ the Lord;"
While yet in chapel, altar, shrine,
The mica in the marble new
Glistened like spangles of the dew.
One minster then was Palestine,
All monumental.
Arculf first
The wonders of the tomb rehearsed,

And Golgotha; then told of trees,
Olives, which in the twilight breeze
Sighed plaintive by the convent's lec
The convent in Gethsemane—
Perished long since. Then: "On the hill—
In site revealed thro' Jesu's grace"—
(Hereat both cross themselves apace)
"A great round church with goodly skill
Is nobly built; and fragrant blows
Morning thro' triple porticoes.
But over that blest place where meet
The last prints of the Wounded Feet,

The roof is open to the sky;

'Tis there the sparrows love to fly.
Upon Ascension Day—at end
Of mass—winds, vocal winds descend
Among the worshipers." Amain
The abbot signs the cross again;
And Arculf on: "And all that night
The mountain temple's western flank—
The same which fronts Moriah's hight—
In memory of the Apostles' light
Shows twelve dyed fires in oriels twelve.
Thither, from towers on Kedron's bank
And where the slope and terrace shelve,
The gathered townsfolk gaze afar;
And those twelve flowers of flame suffuse
Their faces with reflected hues
Of violet, gold, and cinnabar.
Much so from Naples (in our sail
We touched there, shipping jar and bale)
I saw Vesuvius' plume of fire
Redden the bay, tinge mast and spire.
But on Ascension Eve, 'tis then
A light shows—kindled not by men.
Look," pointing to the hearth; "dost see
How these dun embers here by me,
Lambent are licked by flaky flame?
Olivet gleams then much the same—
Caressed, curled over, yea, encurled
By fleecy fires which typic be:
O lamb of God, O light o' the world!"
In fear, and yet a fear divine,
Once more the Culdee made the sign;
Then fervid snatched the palmer's hand—
Clung to it like a very child
Thrilled by some wondrous story wild
Of elf or fay, nor could command
His eyes to quit their gaze at him—
Him who had seen it. But how grim
The Pictish storm-king sang refrain,

Scoffing about those gables high
Over Arculf and good Adamnan.

The abbot and the palmer rest:
The legends follow them and die
Those legends which, be it confessed,
Did nearer bring to them the sky—

Did nearer woo it to their hope
Of all that seers and saints avow—
Than Galileo's telescope
Can bid it unto prosing Science now.

Canto XXXVI - The Tower

The tower they win. Some Greeks at hand,
Pilgrims, in silence view the land.
One family group in listless tone
Are just in act of faring down.
All leave at last. And these remain
As by a hearthstone on the plain
When roof is gone. But can they shame
To tell the evasive thought within?
Does intellect assert a claim
Against the heart, her yielding kin?
But he, the wanderer, the while
See him; and what may so beguile?

Images he the ascending Lord
Pale as the moon which dawn may meet,
Convoyed by a serene accord
And swoon of faces young and sweet—
Mid chaplets, stars, and halcyon wings,
And many ministering things?
As him they mark enkindled so,
What inklings, negatives, they know!
But leaving him in silence due,
They enter there, the print to view—
Affirmed of Christ—the parting foot:

They mark it, nor a question moot;
Next climb the stair and win the roof;
Thence on Jerusalem look down,
And Kedron cringing by the town,
Whose stony lanes map-like were shown.
"Is yon the city Dis aloof?"
Said Rolfe; "nay, liker 'tis some print,
Old blurred, bewrinkled mezzotint.
And distant, look, what lifeless hills!
Dead long for them the hymn of rills
And birds. Nor trees, nor ferns they know;
Nor lichen there hath leave to grow
In baleful glens which blacked the blood
O' the son of Kish."

Far peep they gain
Of waters which in caldron brood,
Sunk mid the mounts of leaden bane:
The Sodom Wave, or Putrid Sea,
Or Sea of Salt, or Cities Five,
Or Lot's, or Death's, Asphaltite,
Or Asafcetida; all these
Being names indeed with which they gyve
That site of foul iniquities
Abhorred.
With wordless look intent,
As if the scene confirmed some thought
Which in heart's lonelier hour was lent,
Vine stood at gaze. The rest were wrought
According unto kind. The Mount
Of Olives, and, in distance there
The charnel wave who may recount?
Hope's hill descries the pit Despair:
Flitted the thought; they nothing said;
And down they drew. As ground they tread,
Nehemiah met them: "Pleaseth ye,
Fair stroll awaits; if all agree,
Over the hill let us go on—
Bethany is a pleasant town.
I'll lead, for well the way I know."

He gazed expectant: Would they go?
Before that simpleness so true
Vine showed embarrassed (Clarel too)
Yet thanked him with a grateful look
Benign; and Rolfe the import took,
And whispered him in softened key,
"Some other day."
And might it be
Such influence their spirits knew
From all the tower had given to view,
Untuned they felt for Bethany?

Canto XXXVII - A Sketch

Not knowing them in very heart,
Nor why to join him they were loth,
He, disappointed, moved apart,
With sad pace creeping, dull, as doth
Along the bough the nerveless sloth.

For ease upon the ground they sit;
And Rolfe, with eye still following
Where Nehemiah slow footed it,
Asked Clarel: "Know you anything
Of this man's prior life at all?"

"Nothing," said Clarel.—"I recall,"
Said Rolfe, "a mariner like him."
"A mariner?"—"Yes; one whom grim
Disaster made as meek as he
There plodding." Vine here showed the zest
Of a deep human interest:
"We crave of you his history."
And Rolfe began: "Scarce would I tell
Of what this mariner befell—
So much is it with cloud o'ercast—
Were he not now gone home at last
Into the green land of the dead,
Where he encamps and peace is shed.

Hardy he was, sanguine and bold,
The master of a ship. His mind
In night-watch frequent he unrolled—
As seamen sometimes are inclined—
On serious topics, to his mate,
A man to creed austere resigned.
The master ever spurned at fate,
Calvin's or Zeno's. Always still
Man-like he stood by man's free will
And power to effect each thing he would,
Did reason but pronounce it good.
The subaltern held in humble way
That still heaven's over-rulings sway
Will and event.
                "On waters far,
Where map-man never made survey,
Gliding along in easy plight,
The strong one brake the lull of night
Emphatic in his willful war—
But staggered, for there came a jar
With fell arrest to keel and speech:
A hidden rock. The pound—the grind—
Collapsing sails o'er deck declined—
Sleek billows curling in the breach,
And nature with her neutral mind.
A wreck. 'Twas in the former days,
Those waters then obscure; a maze;
The isles were dreaded—every chain;

Better to brave the immense of sea,
And venture for the Spanish Main,
Beating and rowing against the trades,
Than float to valleys 'neath the lee,
Nor far removed, and palmy shades.
So deemed he, strongly erring there.
To boats they take; the weather fair—
Never the sky a cloudlet knew;
A temperate wind unvarying blew
Week after week; yet came despair;
The bread tho' doled. and water stored.

Ran low and lower—ceased. They burn—
They agonize till crime abhorred
Lawful might be. O trade-wind, turn!
"Well may some items sleep unrolled—
Never by the one survivor told.
Him they picked up, where, cuddled down,
They saw the jacketed skeleton,
Lone in the only boat that lived—
His signal frittered to a shred.
" 'Strong need'st thou be,' the rescuers said,
'Who has such trial sole survived.'
'I willed it,' gasped he. And the man,
Renewed ashore, pushed off again.
How bravely sailed the pennoned ship
Bound outward on her sealing trip
Antarctic. Yes; but who returns
Too soon, regaining port by land
Who left it by the bay? What spurns
Were his that so could countermand?
Nor mutineer, nor rock, nor gale
Nor leak had foiled him. No; a whale
Of purpose aiming, stove the bow:
They foundered. To the master now
Owners and neighbors all impute
An inauspiciousness. His wife—
Gentle, but unheroic—she,

Poor thing, at heart knew bitter strife
Between her love and her simplicity:
A Jonah is he?—And men bruit
The story. None will give him place
In a third venture. Came the day
Dire need constrained the man to pace
A night patrolman on the quay
Watching the bales till morning hour
Through fair and foul. Never he smiled;

Call him, and he would come; not sour
L In spirit, but meek and reconciled;
Patient he was, he none withstood;
Oft on some secret thing would brood.

He ate what came, though but a crust;
In Calvin's creed he put his trust;
Praised heaven, and said that God was good,
And his calamity but just.
So Silvio Pellico from cell-door
Forth tottering, after dungeoned years,
Crippled and bleached, and dead his peers:
'Grateful, I thank the Emperor.' "

There ceasing, after pause Rolfe drew
Regard to Nehemiah in view:
"Look, the changed master, roams he there?
I mean, is such the guise, the air?"
The speaker sat between mute Vine
And Clarel. From the mystic sea
Laocoon's serpent, sleek and fine,
In loop on loop seemed here to twine
His clammy coils about the three.
Then unto them the wannish man
Draws nigh; but absently they scan;
A phantom seems he, and from zone
Where naught is real tho' the winds aye moan.

Canto XXXVIII - The Sparrow

After the hint by Rolfe bestowed,
Redoubled import, one may ween,
Had Nehemiah's submissive mien
For Clarel. Nay, his poor abode—
And thither now the twain repair—
A new significance might bear.
Thin grasses, such as sprout in sand,
Clarel observes in crannies old
Along the cornice. Not his hand
The mower fills with such, nor arms
Of him that binds the sheaf, enfold.
Now mid the quiet which becharms

That mural wilderness remote,
Querulous came the little note
Of bird familiar—one of them

So numerous in Jerusalem,
Still snared for market, it is told,
And two were for a farthing sold—
The sparrow. But this single one
Plaining upon a terrace nigh,
Was like the Psalmist's making moan
For loss of mate—forsaken quite,
Which on the house-top doth alight
And watches, and her lonely cry
No answer gets.—In sunny hight
Like dotting bees against the sky
What twitterers o'er the temple fly!
But now the arch and stair they gain,
And in the chamber sit the twain.
Clarel in previous time secure,
From Nehemiah had sought to lure
Some mention of his life, but failed.
Rolfe's hintful story so prevailed,
Anew he thought to venture it.
But while in so much else aside
Subject to senile lapse of tide,
In this hid matter of his past
The saint evinced a guardful wit;
His waning energies seemed massed

Here, and but here, to keep the door.
At present his reserve of brow
Reproach in such sort did avow,
That Clarel never pressed him more.
Nay, fearing lest he trespass might
Even in tarrying longer now,
He parted. As he slow withdrew,
Well pleased he noted in review
The hermitage improved in plight.
Some one had done a friendly thing:
Who? Small was Clarel's wondering.

Canto XXXIX - Clarel and Ruth

In northern clime how tender show
The meads beneath heaven's humid Bow
When showers draw off and dew-drops cling
To sunset's skirt, and robins sing
Though night be near. So did the light
Of love redeem in Ruth the trace
Of grief, though scarce might it efface.

From wider rambles which excite
The thought, or study's lone repose,
Daily did Clarel win the close.
With interest feminine and true
The matron watched that love which grew;
She hailed it, since a hope was there
Made brighter for the grief's degree:
How shines the gull ye watch in air
White, white, against the cloud at sea.
Clarel, bereft while still but young,
Mother or sister had not known;
To him now first in life was shown,
In Agar's frank demeanor kind,
What charm to woman may belong
When by a natural bent inclined
To goodness in domestic play:
On earth no better thing than this—
It canonizes very clay:
Madonna, hence thy worship is.
But Ruth: since Love had signed with Fate
The bond, and the first kiss had sealed,
Both for her own and Agar's state
Much of her exile-grief seemed healed:
New vistas opened; and if still
Forebodings might not be forgot
As to her sire's eventual lot,
Yet hope, which is of youth, could thrill.
That frame to foster and defend,
Clarel, when in her presence, strove
The unrest to hide which still could blend

With all the endearings of their love.
Ruth part divined the lurking care,
But more the curb, and motive too:
It made him but love's richer heir;
So much the more attachment grew.
She could not think but all would prove
Subject in end to mighty Love.
That cloud which in the present reigned,
By flushful hope's aurora stained,
At times redeemed itself in hues
Of shell, and humming-bird, and flower.
Could heaven two loyal hearts abuse?
The death-moth, let him keep his bower.

Canto XL - The Mounds

Ere twilight and the shadow fall
On Zion hill without the wall
In place where Latins set the bier
Borne from the gate—who lingers here,
Where, typing faith exempt from loss,
By sodless mound is seen a cross?
Clarel it is, at Celio's grave.
For him, the pale one, ere yet cold,

Assiduous to win and save,
The friars had claimed as of their fold;
Lit by the light of ritual wicks,
Had held to unprotesting lips
In mistimed zeal the crucifix;
And last, among the fellowships
Of Rome's legitimate dead, laid one
Not saved through faith, nor Papal Rome's true son.
Life's flickering hour they made command
Faith's candle in Doubt's dying hand.
So some, who other forms did hold,
Rumored, or criticised, or told
The tale.

Not this did Clarel win
To visit the hermit of the mound.
Nay, but he felt the appeal begin—
The poor petition from the ground:
Remember me! for all life's din
Let not my memory be drowned.
And thought was Clarel's even for one
Of tribe not his—to him unknown
Through vocal word or vital cheer:
A stranger, but less strange made here,
Less distant. Whom life held apart—
Life, whose cross-purposes make shy—
Death yields without reserve of heart
To meditation.
With a sigh
Turning, he slow pursued the steep
Until he won that leveled spot,
Terraced and elevated plot
Over Gihon, where yet others keep
Death's tryst—afar from kindred lie:
Protestants, which in Salem die.
There, fixed before a founded stone
With Bible mottoes part bestrown,
Stood one communing with the bier.

'Twas Rolfe. "Him, him I knew," said he,
Down pointing; "but 'twas far from here—
How far from here!" A pause. "But see,
Job's text in wreath, what trust it giveth;
I KNOW THAT MY REDEEMER LIVETH.
Poor Ethelward! Thou didst but grope;
I knew thee, and thou hadst small hope.
But if at this spent man's death-bed
Some kind soul kneeled and chapter read—
Ah, own! to moderns death is drear,
So drear: we die, we make no sign,
We acquiesce in any cheer—
No rite we seek, no rite decline.
Is't nonchalance of languid sense,
Or the last, last indifference?

With some, no doubt, 'tis peace within;
In others, may be, care for kin:
Exemplary thro' life, as well
Dying they'd be so, nor repel."
He let his eyes half absent move
About the mound: "One's thoughts will rove:
This minds me that in like content,
Other forms were kept without dissent
By one who hardly owned their spell.
He, in fulfillment of pledged work,
Among Turks having passed for Turk,
Sickened among them. On death-bed
Silent he heard the Koran read:
They shrilled the Islam wail for him,
They shawled him in his burial trim;
And now, on brinks of Egypt's waste,
Where the buried Sultans' chapels rise,
Consistently toward Mecca faced,
The blameless simulator lies:
The turbaned Swiss, Sheik Ibrahim—
Burckhardt.—But home the sparrow flees.
Come, move we ere the gate they quit,
And we be shut out here with these
Who never shall re-enter it."

Canto XLI - On the Wall

They parted in the port. Near by,
Long stone stairs win the battlement
Of wall, aerial gallery;

And thither now the student bent
To muse abroad.
The sun's last rays
Shed round a nearing train the haze
Of mote and speck. Advanced in view
And claiming chief regard, came two
Dismounted, barefoot; one in dress
Expressive of deep humbleness

Of spirit, scarce of social state—
His lineaments rebutted that,
Tho' all was overcast with pain—
The visage of a doom-struck man
Not idly seeking holy ground.
Behind, his furnished horse did bound
Checked by a groom in livery fair.
The master paced in act of prayer
Absorbed—went praying thro' the gate.
The attentive student, struck thereat,
The wall crossed—from the inner arch,
Viewed him emerging, while in starch
Of prelate robes, some waiting Greeks
Received him, kissed him on both cheeks,
Showing that specializing love
And deference grave, how far above
What Lazarus in grief may get;
Nor less sincere those priests were yet.
Second in the dismounted list
Was one, a laic votarist,
The cross and chaplet by his side,
Sharing the peace of eventide
In frame devout. A Latin he,
But not, as seemed, of high degree.
Such public reverence profound
In crossing Salem's sacred bound
Is not so common, in late day,
But that the people by the way
In silent-viewing eyes confessed
The spectacle had interest.
Nazarene Hebrews twain rode next,
By one of the escort slyly vexed.
In litter borne by steady mules
A Russian lady parts the screen;
A rider, as the gate is seen,
Dismounts, and her alighting rules—
Her husband. Checkered following there,
Like envoys from all Adam's race,
Mixed men of various nations pace,

I Such as in crowded steamer come
And disembark at Jaffa's stair.
Mute mid the buzz of chat and prayer,
Plain-clad where others sport the plume,
What countrymen are yonder three?
The critic-coolness in their eyes
Disclaims emotion's shallow sea;
Or misapply they precept wise,
Nil admirari? Or, may be,
Rationalists these riders are,
Men self-sufficing, insular.
Nor less they show in grave degree
Tolerance for each poor votary.

Now when the last rays slanting fall,
yhe last new comer enters in:
The gate shuts after with a din.
Tarries the student on the wall.
Dubieties of recent date—
Scenes, words, events—he thinks of all.

As, when the autumn sweeps the down,
And gray skies tell of summer gone,
The swallow hovers by the strait—
Impending on the passage long;
Upon a brink and poise he hung.
The bird in end must needs migrate
Over the sea: shall Clarel too
Launch o'er his gulf, e'en Doubt, and woo
Remote conclusions?
Unresigned,
He sought the inn, and tried to read
|The Fathers with a filial mind.
In vain; heart wandered or repined.
The Evangelists may serve his need:
Deep as he felt the beauty sway,
Estrangement there he could but heed,
Both time and tone so far away
From him the modern. Not to dwell,
Rising he walked the floor, then stood

Irresolute. His eye here fell
Upon the blank wall of the cell,
The wall before him, and he viewed
A place where the last coat of lime—
White flakes whereof lay dropped below—
Thin scaling off, laid open so

Upon the prior coat a rhyme
Pale penciled. In one's nervous trance
Things near will distant things recall,
And common ones suggest romance:
He thought of her built up in wall,
Cristina of Coll'alto; yes,
The verse here breaking from recess—
Tho' immaterial, but a thought
In some sojurning traveler wrought—
Scribbled, overlaid, again revealed—
Seemed like a tragic fact unsealed:
So much can mood possess a man.
He read: obscurely thus it ran:—

"For me who never loved the stride,
Triumph and taunt that shame the winning side—
Toward Him over whom, in expectation's glow,
Elate the advance of rabble-banners gleam—
Turned from a world that dare renounce Him so
My unweaned thoughts in steadfast trade-wind stream.
If Atheists and Vitriolists of doom
Faith's gathering night with rockets red illume—
So much the more in pathos I adore
The low lamps flickering in Syria's Tomb."—

"What strain is this?—But, here, in blur:—
'After return from Sepulcher:
B. L.' "—On the ensuing day
He plied the host with question free:
Who answered him, "A pilgrim—nay,
How to remember! English, though—
A fair young Englishman. But stay:"
And after absence brief he slow

With volumes came in hand: "These, look—
He left behind by chance."—One book,
With portrait of a mitered man,
Treated of high church Anglican,
Confession, fast, saint-day—deplored
That rubric old was not restored.
But under Finis there was writ
A comment that made grief of it.
The second work had other cheer—
Started from Strauss, disdained Renan—
By striding paces up to Pan;
Nor rested, but the goat-god here
Capped with the red cap in the twist
Of Proudhon and the Communist.

But random jottings in the marge
Disclosed some reader of the text
Whose fervid comments did discharge
More dole than e'en dissent. Annexed,
In either book was penciled small:
"B. L.: Oxford: St. Mary's Hall."

Such proved these volumes—such, as scanned
By Clarel, wishful to command
Some hint that might supply a clew
Better enabling to construe
The lines their owner left on wall.

Canto XLII - Tidings

Some of the strangers late arrived
Tarried with Abdon at the inn;
And, ere long, having viewed the town
Would travel further, and pass on
To Siddim, and the Dead Sea win
And Saba. And would Clarel go?
'Twas but for days. They would return
By Bethlehem, and there sojourn

Awhile, regaining Zion so.
But Clarel undetermined stood,
And kept his vacillating mood,
Though learning, as it happed, that Vine
And Rolfe would join the journeying band.
Loath was he here to disentwine
Himself from Ruth. Nor less Lot's land,
And sea, and Judah's utmost drought
Fain would he view, and mark their tone:
And prove if, unredeemed by John,
John's wilderness augmented doubt.
As chanced, while wavering in mind,
And threading a hushed lane or wynd
Quick warning shout he heard behind
And clattering hoofs. He hugged the wall,
Then turned; in that brief interval
The dust came on him, powdery light,
From one who like a javelin flew
Spectral with dust, and all his plight
Charged with the desert and its hue;
A courier, and he bent his flight—
(As Clarel afterward recalled)

Whither lay Agar's close inwalled.
The clank of arms, the clink of shoe,
The cry admonitory too,
Smote him, and yet he scarce knew why;
But when, some hours having flitted by,
Nearing the precincts of the Jew
His host, he did Nehemiah see
Waiting in arch, and with a look
Which some announcement's shadow took,
His heart stood still—Fate's herald, he?
"What is it? what?"—The saint delayed.—
"Ruth?"—"Nathan;" and the news conveyed.
The threat, oft hurled, as oft reviled
By one too proud to give it heed,
The menace of stern foemen wild,
No menace now was, but a deed:
Burned was the roof on Sharon's plain;
And timbers charred showed clotted stain:

But, spirited away, each corse
Unsepulchered remained, or worse.

Ah, Ruth—woe, Agar! Ill breeds ill;
The widow with no future free,
Without resource perhaps, or skill
To steer upon grief's misty sea.
To grieve with them and lend his aid,
Straight to the house see Clarel fare,
The house of mourning—sadder made
For that the mourned one lay not there—
But found it barred. He, waiting so,
Doubtful to knock or call them—lo,
The rabbi issues, while behind
The door shuts to. The meeting eyes
Reciprocate a quick surprise,
Then alter; and the secret mind
The rabbi bears to Clarel shows
In dark superior look he throws:
Censorious consciousness of power:
Death—and it is the Levite's hour.
No word he speaks, but turns and goes.
The student lingered. He was told
By one without, a neighbor old,
That never Jewish modes relent:

Sealed long would be the tenement
To all but Hebrews—of which race
Kneeled comforters by sorrow's side.

So both were cared for. Clogged in pace
He turned away. How pass the tide
Of Ruth's seclusion? Might he gain
Relief from dull inaction's pain?
Yes, join he would those pilgrims now
Which on the morrow would depart
For Siddim, by way of Jericho.
But first of all, he letters sent,
Brief, yet dictated by the heart—
Announced his plan's constrained intent
Reluctant; and consigned a ring
For pledge of love and Ruth's remembering.

Canto XLIII - A Procession

But what!—nay, nay: without adieu
Of vital word, dear presence true,
Part shall I?—break away from love?
But think: the circumstances move,
And warrant it. Shouldst thou abide,
Cut off yet wert thou from her side
For time: tho' she be sore distressed,
Herself would whisper: "Go—'tis best."

Unstable! It was in a street,
Half vault, where few or none do greet,
He paced. Anon, encaved in wall
A fount arrests him, sculpture wrought
After a Saracen design—
Ruinous now and arid all
Save dusty weeds which trail or twine.
While lingering in way that brought
The memory of the Golden Bowl
And Pitcher broken, music rose
Young voices; a procession shows:
A litter rich, with flowery wreath,
Singers and censers, and a veil.
She comes, the bride; but, ah, how pale:
Her groom that Blue-Beard, cruel Death,
Wedding his millionth maid to-day;
She, stretched on that Armenian bier,
Leaves home and each familiar way—
Quits all for him. Nearer, more near—
Till now the ineffectual flame
Of burning tapers borne he saw:
The westering sun puts these to shame.

But, hark: responsive marching choirs,
Robed men and boys, in rhythmic law
A contest undetermined keep:
Ay, as the bass in dolings deep
The serious, solemn thought inspires—
In unconcern of rallying sort

The urchin-treble shrills retort;
But, true to part imposed, again
The beards dirge out. And so they wind
Till thro' the city gate the train
Files forth to sepulcher.
Behind
Left in his hermitage of mind,
What troubles Clarel? See him there
As if admonishment in air
He heard. Can love be fearful so?
Jealous of fate? the future? all
Reverse—mischance? nay, even the pall
And pit?—No, I'll not leave her: no,
'Tis fixed; I waver now no more.—
But yet again he thought it o'er,
And self-rebukeful, and with mock:
Thou superstitious doubter—own,
Biers need be borne; why such a shock
When passes this Armenian one?
The word's dispatched, and wouldst recall?
'Tis but for fleeting interval.

Canto XLIV - The Start

The twilight and the starlight pass,
And breaks the morn of Candlemas.
The pilgrims muster; and they win
A common terrace of the inn,
Which, lifted on Mount Acra's cope,
Looks off upon the town aslope
In gray of dawn. They hear the din
Of mongrel Arabs—the loud coil
And uproar of high words they wage
Harnessing for the pilgrimage.
'Tis special—marks the Orient life,
Which, roused from indolence to toil,
Indignant starts, enkindling strife.
Tho' spite the fray no harm they share,

How fired they seem by burning wrong;

And small the need for strenuous care,
And languor yet shall laze it long.
Wonted to man and used to fate
A pearl-gray ass there stands sedate
While being saddled by a clown
And buffeted. Of her anon.

Clarel regards; then turns his eye
Away from all, beyond the town,
Where pale against the tremulous sky
Olivet shows in morning shy;
Then on the court again looks down.
The mountain mild, the wrangling crew—
In contrast, why should these indue
With vague unrest, and swell the sigh?
Add to the burden? tease the sense
With unconfirmed significance?
To horse. And, passing one by one
Their host the Black Jew by the gate,
His grave salute they take, nor shun
His formal God-speed. One, elate
In air Auroral, June of life,
With quick and gay response is rife.
But he, the Israelite alone,
'Tis he reflects Jehovah's town;
Experienced he, the vain elation gone;
While flit athwart his furrowed face
Glimpses of that ambiguous thought
Which in some aged men ye trace
When Venture, Youth and Bloom go by;
Scarce cynicism, though 'tis wrought
Not all of pity, since it scants the sigh.

They part. Farewell to Zion's seat.
Ere yet anew her place they greet,
In heart what hap may Clarel prove?
Brief term of days, but a profound remove.

END OF FIRST PART

Herman Melville – A Short Biography

Herman Melville was born in New York City on August 1st, 1819, the third of eight children.

At the age of 7 Melville contracted scarlet fever which was to permanently diminish his eyesight. At this time Melville was described as being "very backwards in speech and somewhat slow in comprehension."

Melville attended the Albany Academy from October 1830 to October 1831, where he took the standard preparatory course; reading and spelling; penmanship; arithmetic; English grammar; geography; natural history; universal, Greek, Roman and English history; classical biography; and Jewish antiquities.

The reasons for Melville leaving the Academy after a year are unknown although his brothers continued their education there for a few more months.

In December, Melville's father returned from New York City by steamboat, but difficult weather forced him to travel the last 70 miles in an open carriage in freezing temperatures. A cold developed into delirium and by January 28th, not yet fifty, his father was dead. Melville, at home by now, most probably witnessed much of this event and two decades later he described scenes that must have been very similar in the death of Pierre's father in Pierre.

The family were now in very straitened times. Just 14 Melville took a job in a bank paying $150 a year that he obtained via his uncle, Peter Gansevoort, who was one of the directors of the New York State Bank.

Melville was briefly able to attend again the Albany Academy from October 1836 to March 1837, where he studied the classics.

After a failed stint as a surveyor he signed on to go to sea and travelled across the Atlantic to Liverpool and then on further voyages to the Pacific on adventures which would soon become the architecture of his novels. Whilst travelling he joined a mutiny, was jailed, fell in love with a South Pacific beauty and became known as a figure of opposition to the coercion of native Hawaiians to the Christian religion.

He drew from these experiences in his books Typee, Omoo, and White-Jacket. These were published as novels, the first initially in London in 1846.

They sold very well and enabled him to write full time although royalties were not vast. (During his career it is estimated his writing brought him no more than $10,000)

After a three-month courtship of Elizabeth Shaw, daughter of a prominent Boston family, her father was the Chief Justice of the Massachusetts Supreme Judicial Court, they decided to marry. Her father initially turned down Melville's request but on August 14th, 1847 they married. After initially settling in New York they moved to Massachusetts.

In September of 1850, Melville borrowed $3,000 from his father-in-law Lemuel Shaw to buy a 160-acre farm in Pittsfield. Melville christened the new home 'Arrowhead', due to the quantity of arrowheads dug up around the property during planting season.

That winter, Melville on an impulse paid a visit to the writer Nathaniel Hawthorne. At the time Hawthorne was finishing The House of the Seven Gables and "not in the mood for company". Hawthorne's wife Sophia entertained him while he waited for Hawthorne to come down for supper, and gave him copies of Twice-Told Tales and, The Grandfather's Chair. Melville, sensing a friendship developing, invited them to Arrowhead during the coming weeks. When Sophia agreed, he looked forward to "discussing the Universe with a bottle of brandy & cigars" with Hawthorne.

By 1851 his masterpiece, Moby Dick, was ready to be published. It is perhaps, and certainly at the time, one of the most ambitious novels ever written. However, it never sold out its initial print run of 3,000 and Melville's earnings on this masterpiece were a mere $556.37.

In succeeding years his reputation waned and he found life increasingly difficult. His family was growing, now four children, and a stable income was essential.

From 1853 to 1856, Melville began to publish his short stories in the growing magazine market, most notably "Bartleby, the Scrivener" (1853), "The Encantadas" (1854), and "Benito Cereno" (1855). These and others were later collected together and published in 1856 as the Plazza Tales.

In 1857, he travelled to England where, for the first time since 1852, he reunited with Hawthorne. He then went on to tour the Near East. The Confidence-Man was the last prose work that he published that same year. It received little attention.

With his finances in a disappointing state Melville took the advice of friends that a change in career was called for. For many others public lecturing had proved very rewarding. From late 1857 to 1860, Melville embarked upon three lecture tours, where he spoke mainly on Roman statuary and sightseeing in Rome. These lectures mocked the pseudo-intellectualism of lyceum culture. His words though were ignored by contemporary audiences.

In the 1860's he wrote many poems, many based on the Civil War. But there was no publisher for him and no audience.

In 1866, Melville's wife and her relatives used their influence to obtain a position for him as customs inspector for the City of New York, With his writings almost ignored they moved to New York where Melville joined the New York Customs house and worked there for the next 19 years.

For Melville his early promise and great talents seemed to be getting him nowhere in literary terms. Despite periods of drinking, depression and other ails Elizabeth stood by her husband despite calls from other family members and the marriage held together.

In 1876 he was at last able to publish privately his 16,000 line epic poem Clarel, in which a young American student of divinity travels to Jerusalem to renew his faith. It was to no avail. The book had an initial printing of 350 copies, but sales failed miserably, and the unsold copies were burned when Melville was unable to afford to buy them at cost.

On December 31st, 1885 Melville was at last able to retire. His wife had inherited several small legacies and with her astute ways it was enough to provide them with a reasonable income and Melville had enough to buy further precious books and supplies.

In these last few years Melville finished two poetry collections which were printed privately, although only 25 copies of each; John Marr and Other Sailors (1888) and Timoleon (1891).

Herman Melville, novelist, poet, short story writer and essayist, died at his home on September 28rh 1891 from cardiovascular disease.

He was interred in the Woodlawn Cemetery in The Bronx, New York City.

He was the first writer to have his works collected and published by the Library of America.

Herman Melville – A Concise Bibliography

Novels, Short Stories & Poetry

Typee: A Peep at Polynesian Life (1846)
Omoo: A Narrative of Adventures in the South Seas (1847)
Mardi: And a Voyage Thither (1849)
Redburn: His First Voyage (1849)
White-Jacket; or, The World in a Man-of-War (1850)
Moby-Dick; or, The Whale (1851)
Pierre: or, The Ambiguities (1852)
Isle of the Cross (1853 unpublished, and now lost)
Cock-A-doodle-Doo (Short story) (1852)
Bartleby, the Scrivener (Short story) (1853)
The Encantadas, or Enchanted Isles (Short story) (1854)
Poor Man's Pudding and Rich Man's Crumbs (Short story) (1854)
The Happy Failure (Short story) (1854)
The Lightning-Rod Man (Short story) (1854)
The Fiddler (Short story) (1854)
Benito Cereno (1855)
Israel Potter: His Fifty Years of Exile (1855)
The Paradise of Batchelors and the Tartarus of Maids (Short story) (1855)
The Bell-Tower (Short story) (1855)
Jimmy Rose (Short story) (1855)
The Gees (Short story) (1856)
I and My Chimney (Short story) (1856)
The Apple-Tree Story (Short story) (1856)
The Confidence-Man: His Masquerade (1857)
The Piazza (Short story) (1856)
Battle-Pieces and Aspects of the War (Poetry) (1866)
Clarel: A Poem and Pilgrimage in the Holy Land (Epic poem) (1876)
John Marr and Other Sailors (Poetry) (1888)
Timoleon (Poetry) (1891)
Billy Budd, Sailor (An Inside Narrative) (1891 unfinished, published posthumously in 1924)

Essays

Fragments from a Writing Desk, No. 1 (May 4, 1839)
Fragments from a Writing Desk, No. 2 (May 18, 1839)
Etchings of a Whaling Cruise (1847)
Authentic Anecdotes of 'Old Zack" (July 24 to September 11, 1847)
Mr Parkman's Tour (March 31, 1849)
Cooper's New Novel (April 28, 1849)
A Thought on Book-Binding (March 16, 1850)
Hawthorne and His Mosses (August 17 and August 24, 1850)

www.ingramcontent.com/pod-product-compliance
Lightning Source LLC
Chambersburg PA
CBHW060117050426
42448CB00010B/1911